W9-AJK-958

The Atlas of the
RENAISSANCE
WORLD

**McGraw-Hill
Children's Publishing**

A Division of The **McGraw·Hill** *Companies*

This edition published in the United States in 2003
by Peter Bedrick Books,
an imprint of McGraw-Hill Children's Publishing,
a Division of the McGraw-Hill Companies
8787 Orion Place, Columbus, OH 43240

www.MHkids.com

ISBN 0-87226-692-3

Library of Congress Cataloging-in-Publication Data is on file with the publisher.

The Atlas of the Renaissance World was created and produced by
McRae Books Srl, via de' Rustici, 5 – Florence (Italy)
info@mcraebooks.com

Publishers: Anne McRae, Marco Nardi
Text: Neil Grant
Illustrations: Gian Luigi Albertini, Paola Baldanzi, Lorenzo Cecchi, Luisa Della Porta, Lucia Mattioli,
Paola Ravaglia, Studio Stalio (Alessandro Cantucci, Fabiano Fabbrucci, Andrea Morandi, Ivan Stalio)
Photos: pages 16, 19, 36 Scala Group, Florence
Picture Research: Loredana Agosta
Graphic Design: Marco Nardi
Editing: Loredana Agosta, Anne McRae
US Editors: Joanna Schmalz, Tracy Paulus, Andrea Pelleschi
Layout and Cutouts: Laura Ottina, Filippo Delle Monache
Color Separations: Litocolor, Florence

Printed in the Slovak Republic
1 2 3 4 5 6 7 8 9 10 MCR 07 06 05 04 03 02

THE ATLAS OF THE
RENAISSANCE
WORLD

Neil Grant

Illustrations Paola Ravaglia, Studio Stalio (Fabiano Fabbrucci,
Alessandro Cantucci, Andrea Morandi, Ivan Stalio), Luisa Della Porta

PETER BEDRICK BOOKS

Contents

Christianity and antiquity

The deep admiration of Renaissance scholars and artists for the culture of antiquity posed one problem. The ancient Greeks and Romans, whose civilization seemed so much more advanced than their own, were not Christians. Early Renaissance humanists spent a great deal of effort trying to reconcile Christianity with the pagan beliefs of the ancients (St. Augustine had tackled the same question a thousand years earlier). Although they were not tempted to question Christianity, their minds were no longer ruled by the authority and rigid teaching of the Church.

The ancient concept of the wheel of fortune, controlled by the fickle goddess Fortuna, appealed to the Renaissance more than the medieval idea of all things being subject to the will of God.

Hercules and the Hydra (about 1470), by Antonio Pollaiuolo, of Florence. The Hydra was a many-headed monster which, when one head was cut off, grew two more (killing one enemy creates more).

Above: Wood carving of three putti (cupids) playing, by Hans Daucher, about 1530. Cupids were a feature of Classical art, adopted by Italian and later by northern artists.

The human being

The medieval Church placed God at the center of the universe and treated human beings as wretched creatures striving to obey God's will in hope of a better life after death. The Renaissance philosophy of humanism, while it did not reject God, put the human being at the center of the universe. In art, this showed itself in the new popularity of the portrait, and in the efforts of artists to treat their subjects with realism and passion.

Leonardo's relaxed portrait of a young courtier, Cecilia Gallerani. The ermine (so real, people want to touch it) is a play on her name, which is close to the Greek word for ermine.

Myth and allegory

The stories of gods and heroes from Greek and Roman mythology were often used by Renaissance artists. Such works often took the form of allegory, in which the images contain a hidden message, and the figures represent abstract qualities such as liberty, justice, or greed. It was (and is) usually necessary to know the original story or myth to understand the meaning.

Renaissance music

Most medieval music was religious, but Renaissance music covered a much wider range. Music was a standard subject of education and most people could sing and play the lute, the Renaissance equivalent of the guitar. Music and dance were part of public life and, increasingly, of home life too. Even the ships of the discoverers carried trumpets and drums. Printed music became available in 1501, and new forms appeared, such as the madrigal.

Viols, played with a bow, developed during the Renaissance, but were soon superseded by the violin family.

Introduction

European history is roughly divided into three periods: Ancient (Greeks and Romans), Medieval, and Modern. The Renaissance marks the end of the Middle Ages and the beginning of the Modern Age, and occupies, roughly, the 15th and 16th centuries. Our word "renaissance" comes from a French word meaning rebirth. It refers to the revival and recovery of the art, literature, and ideas of ancient Greece and Rome. The study of antiquity encouraged a new interest in the world of nature and the individual. A new spirit of human enterprise and curiosity about the world was born. It stimulated, and was in turn stimulated by, further developments: the religious Reformation, which broke the monopoly of the Roman Church, and the voyages of discovery, which revealed new continents and peoples, and proved that all the seas and oceans are connected.

By the time the Ottoman Turks captured Constantinople (above), the Europeans had learned more of ancient Greek scholarship from Arabic translations.

Michelangelo's statue of David (1501–1504), the slayer of Goliath. It was carved from a single block of marble.

Renaissance art and architecture

The word *rinascimento* (Italian for "rebirth") was first applied to painting. The 16th century art historian Vasari used it to describe the return to the realistic, ancient Roman style of painting practiced by Giotto (died 1337) who is regarded as a founder of modern painting. In fact, the Classical tradition, which was overwhelmed by the medieval Gothic style of art and architecture in most of Europe, was never completely broken in Italy. The Classical style of antiquity was not simply copied in the Renaissance. Architects, for instance, borrowed all the devices of their ancient predecessors, yet their buildings clearly belong to the Renaissance, not ancient Rome.

Left: A Roman capital of a column from Brunelleschi's Ospedale degli Innocenti (see page 8).

Coral, on a silver-gilt stand, obtained during a war with the Ottoman Turks and presented to Florence Cathedral, 1447.

The fall of Constantinople

Although the Roman empire in the west collapsed in the 5th century, the Eastern, or Byzantine, empire, based in Constantinople, existed until 1453. The Byzantines never forgot their Roman origins, but the religious split between the Roman and the Byzantine Greek Orthodox Churches ensured that East and West stayed divided. Some contacts continued, especially with Venice, and the little that Europeans knew of ancient Greek culture came partly from Byzantine scholars. The fall of Constantinople (1453) sent more Greek scholars and manuscripts to Europe and contributed to the development of the Renaissance.

Below: A dragon from one of the gates of the imperial palace of the Ming emperors in Beijing. Europeans craved Chinese products such as pottery and silks.

A page, in Greek type, of a book on philosophy printed in Venice in 1500.

Printing

A striking feature of the Renaissance was the greater speed of change. Ideas could not have spread so fast without the invention, about 1455, of printing with movable metal type. Previously, books only existed in manuscript, and each book had to be copied by hand, making books rare and expensive. Printing allowed hundreds of copies to be produced in less time than one copy of a manuscript.

The Reformation

In the early 16th century, the monopoly of the 1,000-year-old Roman Church over Western Christianity was broken, and many Protestant Churches were established that denied the authority of the Pope. This was a crisis of the Church as an institution, not of Christianity, for this was a very religious age. The Reformation had a marked effect on culture. It encouraged everyday languages instead of Latin, for instance, in translations of the Bible. Its effect on the arts was more mixed. Most Protestants disliked, and even destroyed, the works of art that adorned medieval churches.

The culture of the rich

In Renaissance times the arts and literature depended not only on the existence of brilliant artists and writers, but also on rich patrons to employ them. A man like Duke Federico de Montefeltro was both a professional general and ruler of Urbino and a man of great taste and refinement. The power of a ruler or the wealth of a banker was demonstrated in beautiful possessions and lavish entertainments.

Right: A gold coin bearing an image of the Pope, who was a political figure in the Renaissance. He was more prince than priest, which alienated religious reformers.

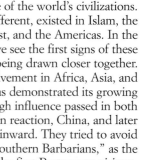

Left: A bronze candlestick in the form of a court jester. Many courts employed such a licensed clown, whose only job was to keep people amused.

World civilizations

Europe was just one of the world's civilizations. Others, very different, existed in Islam, the Far East, and the Americas. In the Renaissance we see the first signs of these civilizations being drawn closer together. Europe's involvement in Africa, Asia, and the Americas demonstrated its growing powers, though influence passed in both directions. In reaction, China, and later Japan, turned inward. They tried to avoid people like the "Southern Barbarians," as the Chinese called the first Portuguese visitors.

Italian Origins

The Renaissance began in the cities of northern Italy, although it is hard to say exactly when. Signs of change can be traced back for centuries, but it was not until the 14th century that ordinary men began to study the literature and art of ancient Rome. Within a few years, the universities were dominated by scholars of Latin and the classics. These men were later called "humanists." The new learning captured the imagination of princes and merchants, and artists worked in a recognizable "Renaissance" style. The reasons for this blossoming of culture lay in the growth of the Italian city-states. They had developed into communes or republics, ruled by merchants and businessmen who had grown rich in trade and banking. Cities such as Florence, Genoa, Milan, and Venice were rich and powerful and independent too, for the powers that dominated medieval Italy, the Holy Roman Emperor and the Papacy, were much weaker in the 14th century.

Above: Italy in the 14th century. Northern Italy was divided into more than 20 states. The Kingdom of Naples occupied the poorer south, with the Papal States in the center.

The Palazzo Pubblico in Siena, seat of government and symbol of city pride.

Guelphs and Ghibellines

In the 13th century, the sharpest conflict in Italy was between the supporters of the Pope (Guelphs) and the supporters of the Holy Roman emperor (Ghibellines) in the struggle for control of Italy. As time went on, that conflict faded and merged with local quarrels between rival groups and families, although some cities always remained Guelph and others Ghibelline.

*Above: Seal of Guelphs.
Right: Seal of the Ghibellines.*

The republics

From the 11th century, many northern Italian cities formed themselves into communes and republics, led by a council of businessmen. Some were quite democratic, although many soon fell under the control of a powerful family, like the Medici in Florence. The people had great pride in their city, rather than in any larger region, and they built grand civic buildings in its honor.

Below: Records are carefully checked at a meeting of businessmen concluding a deal.

Business and banking

Northern Italy, especially the area from Tuscany to Venice, was the most prosperous part of Europe in the 15th century, thanks to trade, the wool industry, and banking. Banking had disappeared in medieval Europe because the Church forbade lending money at interest, but booming Italian trade revived it in the 14th century. The Medici bank in Florence had the Pope and the king of France among its customers.

Maritime republics

Trade was a major source of wealth, and the chief trading states were Venice and Genoa. Venice was the richest state and one of the most powerful in Europe. It benefited from its position on the Adriatic Sea, and had colonies in the Greek islands and even, for a time, Cyprus. It controlled most of the trade in luxuries from the East, such as silk and spices. Genoa was its greatest rival, but after 1380 its influence was reduced by defeat in war.

Patronage of wealthy merchants

Pride in their city inspired rich men to spend on art and buildings, not only for themselves, but also for the city. The building above, an orphanage (Ospedale degli Innocenti), was built by the great architect of Florence, Brunelleschi, in the 1420s. It was paid for by a wealthy merchant, Francesco Datini, himself an orphan.

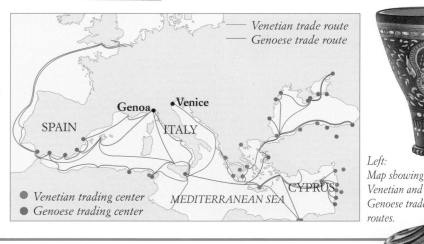

— Venetian trade route
— Genoese trade route

● Venetian trading center
● Genoese trading center

Left: Map showing Venetian and Genoese trade routes.

Above and left: A 15th-century map of Venice and an example of its most famous product, glass.

Below: Statue of Bartolommeo Colleoni (1400–1475), a fierce commander of mercenaries in the service of Venice.

War and conflict

In spite of its prosperity, beautiful buildings, and works of art, early Renaissance Italy was not a peaceful country. Every state was in conflict with its neighbors. While at home, rival families struggled for power, sometimes hiring private armies. These feuds could bring ruin. Perugia was torn by war and riots for four years, 100 men were hanged in one day, and troops camped in the cathedral. The city never fully recovered.

Above: Rival bands of Guelphs and Ghibellines fighting on the walls of Florence (the building behind is the Baptistery).

Fortified cities

War was a common fact of life in the 15th century. Every community was surrounded by rivals or enemies and threatened by bandits, rogue mercenaries, or foreign invaders. Not surprisingly, cities looked like fortresses, whose towers sometimes served as private forts for rival parties.

Civic pride

Citizens' pride in their cities was expressed not only in palaces and civic buildings, but in a more traditional way in its churches. The greatest glory of Florence was its cathedral, started as early as 1296 but completed, with Brunelleschi's famous dome, in the 15th century. Citizens of all classes contributed to the building of the cathedral.

Despots

In the 15th century some of the Italian states were still republics with a semi-democratic government (though not many citizens could vote). As time passed, the richest families gained more power for themselves, and sometimes one man took over the government. Not all these despots, or tyrants, were bad rulers. Many were good governors, generous patrons of the arts, and devoted to the state.

Right: Sigismondo Malatesta, duke of Rimini (1417–1468), prays to his patron saint, St. Sigismund. His family were Guelphs, who came to power by driving out the Ghibellines but were themselves driven out in 1500.

Left: The bell tower of Florence cathedral was the voice of the city that in times of danger called citizens to man the gates and walls.

The sign or trademark, of the wool merchants' guild in Florence, by Luca della Robbia.

The guilds

The guilds were associations of men of a given trade, such as wool merchants, bankers, lawyers, or doctors, that controlled their own trades or business and supported their members and their families. They even had their own church. In many cities, the larger guilds grew powerful. Officers of the leading guilds often served in the government.

Right: This panel, The Sacrifice of Isaac by Ghiberti, won the competition for the doors of the Baptistery.

Right: Once a year, the wool merchants' guild in Florence gave out free clothing to the poor, including children.

The guilds as patrons

The guilds, like wealthy citizens and rulers, supported charities and the arts as part of their civic duty. In Florence, they commissioned many fine sculptures that can now be seen in their former church. The wool merchants sponsored a competition for the design of double bronze doors for the Baptistery of Florence cathedral.

Right: This sculpture of St. George by Donatello was commissioned by the guild of armorers and sword makers.

Left: A bronze relief of St. Zenobius in the Palazzo Vecchio or Florentine town hall, is now in the Bargello, a national museum.

Patron saints

The weakening of the Church and the new spirit of humanism among educated people did not mean that religion was a less serious matter. The church was still the center of the community, and people had not lost their devotion to the local saints. Every community and guild had its own patron saint. A revered figure in Florence was St. Zenobius, who had been its bishop in the 4th century and was said to have performed miracles.

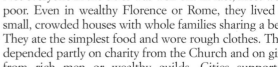

Charity

Not everyone in the cities was well-off. In fact, most were poor. Even in wealthy Florence or Rome, they lived in small, crowded houses with whole families sharing a bed. They ate the simplest food and wore rough clothes. They depended partly on charity from the Church and on gifts from rich men or wealthy guilds. Cities supported hospitals, alms houses, and children's homes.

Trade, Banking, and Agriculture

The 14th century was a disastrous time in Europe, marked by epidemics, famine, and peasant rebellions, as well as the usual wars. Yet some signs of economic recovery appeared even before 1400. Farming methods were improving in some regions, especially northern Italy. Wasteland was cleared for crops, and in parts of Germany new settlements were cut out of the forests. Labor was more flexible. Peasants took on more responsibilities, and farming became more specialized. Farmers responded to increasing demands for meat, and drove on roads that linked the meat producers with the towns. More vineyards were planted, and grain, especially wheat, was grown by more systematic methods, especially near towns. With population growing again, demand for food, and also for wool, rose, and the cloth industry expanded rapidly, especially in Italy.

French peasants making hay.

80 millions				
70				
60				
50				
40				
30				
20				
10	1200	1300	1347	1352

This chart shows how Europe's population, rising in the 13th century, fell sharply after the plague.

Agricultural improvements

In 1300 farming was primitive, with most people growing their own food. With the population growing again, especially in towns, farming revived in the 15th century. Improved methods increased the food supply and led to wider markets. Important improvements were the three-field system (in which land did not have to be left fallow every year or two), and a heavier plow with an iron plowshare that turned the soil, rather than just breaking it up.

There was no shortage of wheat in the Florence grain market.

The decline of feudalism

Falling population, aggravated by the Black Death, caused a shortage of labor. Serfdom, in which people worked for and were to some extent "owned" by their lord, was already fading away. Farm workers became paid laborers. Plenty of fertile land lay uncultivated, and some peasants became small farmers. However, these advantages did not prevent frequent peasant rebellions against landlords.

After the Black Death

In 1348 an epidemic of a disease called the plague reached Italy. It swept across Europe in two years, killing one-third of the population. Whole villages were wiped out. This horror, known as the Black Death, was the worst disaster in European history.

Above: Turning wool into cloth involved many different crafts, ending with this final brush-up.

Left: A weaver at work. The horizontal loom was more versatile than the vertical loom, but it took up more space and required more skill.

The textile industry

Cloth-making was by far the biggest industry and the main driving force of international trade. Wool produced in England, for example, was made into cloth in Flanders, Belgium (until the English began to make it themselves), and perhaps sold in a third country. Also, the Italian cloth industry used wool from the much-admired Merino sheep in Spain.

Below: Shipbuilding in Venice.

Recovery of trade

Trade also began to recover in the 15th century, though another century passed before it reached the scale of the prosperous 13th century. Italian merchants, especially, were big businessmen, who seldom traveled abroad themselves but had representatives in foreign ports. Trading was made easier by the rising supply of money and the use of bills of exchange (predecessors of checks).

Shipbuilding

Medieval sailors tried to stay as close to the coast as possible. But advances in shipbuilding, such as the rudder, made long ocean voyages possible in the 15th century. A big improvement came from mixing the northern tradition of sturdy, stubby, square-sailed vessels with the southern tradition of lighter hulls and lateen rig (triangular sails). From the first came strength and power before the wind; from the second came greater mobility and easier sailing in unfavorable winds.

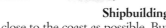

Imports and exports

All industry was small-scale. Although Florence had only 200 big cloth merchants, they had no large factories. They were more like managers, using the services of hundreds of mostly small workshops. Trade was a two-way business. A German merchant might export northern goods like timber, furs, and fish, while importing wine and cloth from the south.

A window from Chartres cathedral, France, showing fur merchants.

Currency

Trade was profitable, but risky. One of the problems was exchanging money. A huge variety of different currencies existed. There were nearly 400 different coins in the Netherlands alone. There were printed tables giving exchange values, but they were often unreliable. The value of a coin depended on the amount of silver or gold it contained. The reason the Florentine florin (left) was so widely used was that its value was reliable.

This map shows the mines in use by the mid-15th century.

Mining

Mining was considered a good investment. Demand for weapons and tools led to an expansion of iron mining: the iron mines at Schwaz in Austria alone employed about 20,000 people. More valuable was silver. People believed that the wealth of a country, or person, was measured by the amount of treasure it, or he, possessed, and the discovery of the German silver mines, and later others in Bohemia and Poland, was one of the causes of business prosperity in the 13th century.

Right: Better pumps and winches enabled the German silver miners to descend 984 feet (300 meters) into the earth.

Left: Bankers in Perugia with some female customers.

Below: Merchant Francesco Datini thanks God for making him rich.

Arms of the Bardi (below) and of Peruzzi, leading bankers.

The Hanseatic League

Trade in northern Europe was dominated by the cities of the Hanseatic League. The League, founded in Lübeck and Hamburg in 1241, was composed of nearly 100 cities in the 14th century. It acted like an independent power and had its own army and navy. Some members gave their loyalty to the League rather than their local ruler. The League traded in wool, textiles, and silver, among other goods.

Above: An early Renaissance safe.

Right: Jacob Fugger discusses business with a clerk.

Banking

The first bankers in the Middle Ages were simply money lenders, usually Jews, who did not have to obey the Church's ban on usury (lending money at interest). By the 14th century, banking in the leading commercial cities had become more advanced and profitable. When the Peruzzi, leading Italian bankers, went bankrupt in the 1340s, the impact was felt throughout Europe.

Banking families

Like most trades and professions, banking was hereditary: sons followed fathers. Some families became very rich and well known. The Peruzzi were the biggest family, until the king of England bankrupted them by not paying his debts. They were even bigger than the Medici. In Germany, the greatest firms were the Fuggers, bankers to the Holy Roman Emperor, and their rivals, the Welsers.

Below: The wealthy Enrico Scrovegni presents a model of the chapel to the Virgin of Charity that he built to atone for making profits by usury in 1302.

Map showing the Hanseatic League and major banking families.

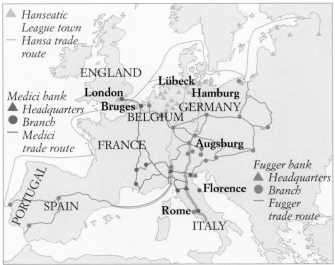

- ▲ Hanseatic League town
- — Hansa trade route
- ▲ Medici bank Headquarters
- ● Branch
- — Medici trade route
- ▲ Fugger bank Headquarters
- ● Branch
- — Fugger trade route

Patronage of wealthy bankers

In a play by Ben Jonson, a miser named Volpone exclaims, "My gold! Open the shrine that I may see my saint." But bankers were not supposed to think only of their profits, they were expected to give generously to the Church, the city, and the poor. Many did, but they were widely suspected, especially by the Church (and sometimes rightly), of worshiping money to such an extent that they undermined Christian society.

Above: A Renaissance illustration showing the poet Dante being expelled from Florence.

Early humanists

The first Renaissance humanist was the Italian poet and scholar Petrarch (1304–1374). Besides his love of poetry, the model for future poets, he strived to bridge the gap between Christian beliefs and the morality of the Ancients. Other important figures were Petrarch's friend and follower, Boccaccio (1313–1375), author of the *Decameron*, who was also influenced by Dante (1265–1321), the first "modern" poet.

Above: Boccaccio with his book of stories. The early humanists wrote in their native language, not Latin.

Left: The spirit of inquiry: scholars journeying along the path to knowledge (1505, from Siena cathedral).

Classical Antiquity and Humanism

The greatest change that took place in the Renaissance was a change in attitude, a new way of looking at the world. This outlook came to be called humanism. It began with the study of the works of antiquity, the Classical world of Greece and Rome, by scholars. In Latin (ancient Roman) writings, they discovered a fund of knowledge and experience of which little had been known during the Middle Ages. But those ancient writers had been non-Christians, and in many ways their writings contradicted the teachings of the Church. Yet on most other matters, from politics to art, the ideas of the Ancients seemed far advanced. Gradually the education and outlook of Europeans changed, as Classical antiquity became the basis of standards of learning and art.

Quest for knowledge

Early humanists, while loyal to the Christian Church, could see the virtues of the Classical world, in which Christianity was irrelevant. They studied all the works they could obtain, searched out new ones, and had Greek works translated into Latin (or learned Greek themselves; all educated people knew Latin, which was also the language of the Church). The ancient scholars often seemed far wiser than themselves, but they shared their spirit of curiosity and inquiry about the world, which the medieval Church discouraged.

Left: An illustration of the liberal arts, with the most important subjects of theology and philosophy, at the center.

Education

Except for boys entering the Church or studying law or medicine, education was limited. It provided basic, necessary skills like reading and writing. However, without altering the basic system, humanist scholars such as Pico della Mirandola injected more lively debate and encouraged students to think, not just learn. A dog, said Pico, behaves always like a dog, but people can direct their own development.

Above: Petrarch at work in his study.

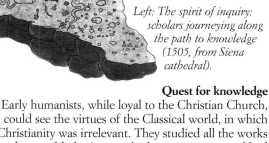

- Milan Verona Padua Venice
- Pavia Mantua
  Ferrara
- Genoa Bologna
  Lucca Montecatini Rimini
  Empoli Florence
  Arezzo
  Siena
  Todi

☐ Area controlled by Florence in 1492 Rome

Crown of laurel

A crown of laurel leaves, as worn here by Dante, was a mark of honor and distinction. Universities gave it to graduates in certain subjects and to outstanding poets. Early humanists sometimes established close and inspiring relationships with long-dead Classical predecessors, such as Dante with Virgil, and Petrarch with Cicero.

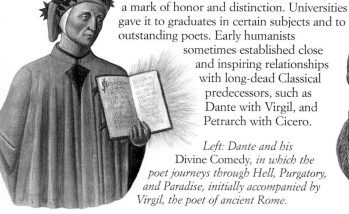

Left: Dante and his Divine Comedy, in which the poet journeys through Hell, Purgatory, and Paradise, initially accompanied by Virgil, the poet of ancient Rome.

The map shows early centers of humanist studies in Italy. Because so many leading writers came from Tuscany, the Tuscan dialect became the standard version of Italian.

Left: Teacher and students. Learning in most schools was still by rote.

Humanism

The medieval Church put God at the center of the universe and regarded human life only as preparation for the life to come. The Church decided what was good and what was sinful and allowed no disagreement. Humanism, which was established around 1500, made human beings central. Humanists refused to accept everything the Church taught without question. But they had no single philosophy, and though they criticized the Church, most remained good Christians.

Detail from a Botticelli painting: The Renaissance prince Lorenzo de Medici with two humanist scholars.

Religion and Humanism

There were problems in bringing together Christian civilization and non-Christian Antiquity. Christian explanations were sometimes contradicted by Classical learning. Classical thinkers had different ideas on, for example, how the earth was created, than Christians, who believed the creation story in the Bible. In general, humanism encouraged an independent, individual, and critical outlook. This was a threat to the universal authority claimed by the Church.

Above: Page from a book by Marsilio Ficino, a scholar who combined Christian belief with the philosophy of Plato.

Right: Botticelli's Venus *illustrates how painters also sought a Platonic ideal form.*

Above: St. Jerome, an early father of the Church, was admired by humanists because he was a Classical scholar as well as a Christian saint.

Imitation of Classical art

The style of art in the Renaissance was derived from ancient Greece and Rome. Like Classical art, it was realistic, in the sense that the artwork looked like the subject. It was also influenced by the ancient Greek Platonic idea of ideal form.

This 16th century bronze figure of Apollo was based on a marble statue from ancient Rome, itself a copy of an earlier Greek work.

Revival of Classical Antiquity

Renaissance humanism was not just a renewed interest in Classical Antiquity (ancient Greece and Rome). The ancient world had never been entirely forgotten during the Middle Ages, and there had been revivals of Classical learning before. But the research of humanist scholars revealed a huge civilization, in many ways like their own, that had covered a continent and lasted for centuries. Its writers spoke clearly to them, almost like friends and helped to open up people's minds.

Neoplatonism

Neoplatonism was a philosophy based on the writings of Plato, the premier philosopher of Classical Greece, as interpreted by Plotinus in the 3rd century A.D. It was revived in the 15th century in the Florentine Academy, whose director was Marsilio Ficino. Important aspects of Neoplatonism were the concept of the unity, goodness, and holiness of the universe, and that beyond the material universe there is a greater reality. These ideas attracted religious thinkers.

Writing equipment from the desk of a humanist scholar.

Below: A 15th century painting of Famous Men, *includes this portrait of Plato (427–347 B.C.).*

Manuscripts and libraries

Classical literature was the basis for Renaissance humanism, and scholars eagerly tracked down manuscripts and books. Some were retranslated from Arabic. Another source was Byzantium (Constantinople), which fell to the Ottoman Turks in 1453, with many scholars fleeing to the West. No cultured man was without his library. Federico da Montefeltro, duke of Urbino, employed over 30 scribes to copy manuscripts.

In the 15th century, cultured Italian princes often owned libraries.

A 16th century collector, painted by Titian, proudly displays a figure of Venus, the Roman goddess of love.

Collecting antiquities

Artists studied antiquities, seeking out examples from the ruins of Rome and other places. In time, every cultured man became a collector of antiquities, especially of sculpture but also of other things, such as coins and minerals. Interest in Classical art soon led wealthy patrons to commission work from promising artists of their own day.

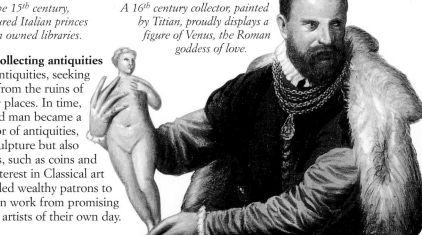

Florence and the Medici

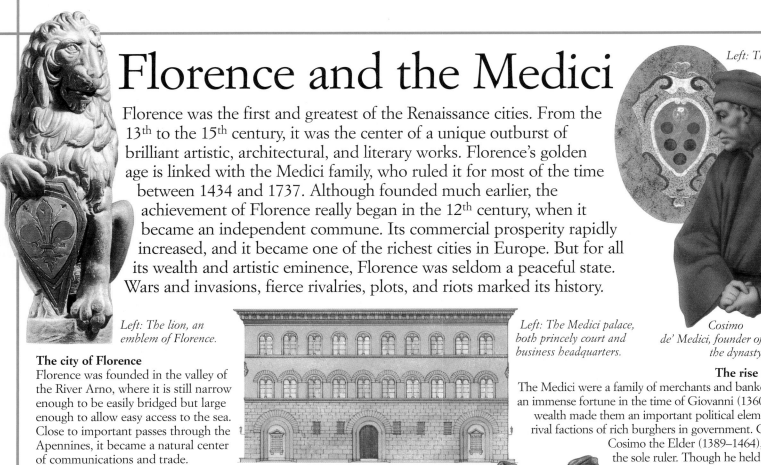

Left: The Medici coat of arms.

Florence was the first and greatest of the Renaissance cities. From the 13th to the 15th century, it was the center of a unique outburst of brilliant artistic, architectural, and literary works. Florence's golden age is linked with the Medici family, who ruled it for most of the time between 1434 and 1737. Although founded much earlier, the achievement of Florence really began in the 12th century, when it became an independent commune. Its commercial prosperity rapidly increased, and it became one of the richest cities in Europe. But for all its wealth and artistic eminence, Florence was seldom a peaceful state. Wars and invasions, fierce rivalries, plots, and riots marked its history.

Left: The lion, an emblem of Florence.

Left: The Medici palace, both princely court and business headquarters.

Cosimo de' Medici, founder of the dynasty.

The city of Florence
Florence was founded in the valley of the River Arno, where it is still narrow enough to be easily bridged but large enough to allow easy access to the sea. Close to important passes through the Apennines, it became a natural center of communications and trade.

Below: The Piazza Santa Croce, where games, contests, and jousting took place.

Right: Part of Gozzoli's paintings from the chapel of the Medici palace showing Medici portraits: Cosimo and his son Piero.

The rise of the Medici
The Medici were a family of merchants and bankers, who made an immense fortune in the time of Giovanni (1360–1429). Their wealth made them an important political element among the rival factions of rich burghers in government. Giovanni's son, Cosimo the Elder (1389–1464), made himself the sole ruler. Though he held no high office and insisted he was merely a citizen of the republic, he sent rivals into exile and controlled city officials.

The Medici as art patrons
Cosimo the Elder and his successors were generous patrons of artists and architects. Most of the Renaissance buildings of Florence, including the cathedral, owe something to the Medici. Their reasons were partly political and partly personal. Such generosity made them popular, but they were also cultured men and keen scholars, devoted to the arts.

Below: A view of Florence about 1480.

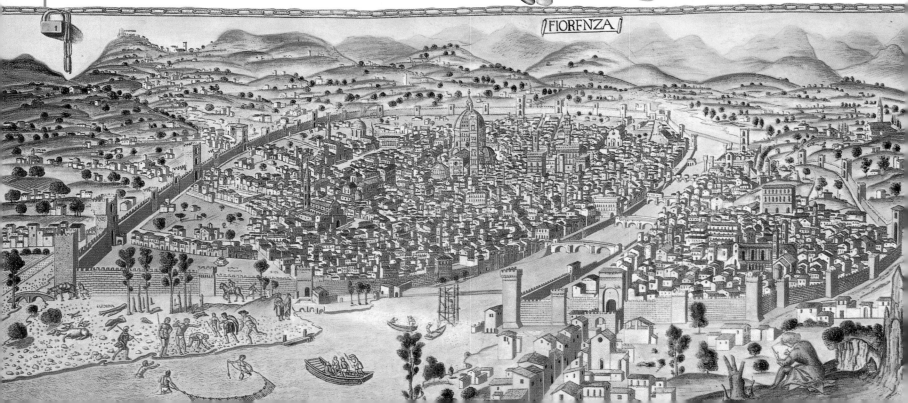

FIORENZA

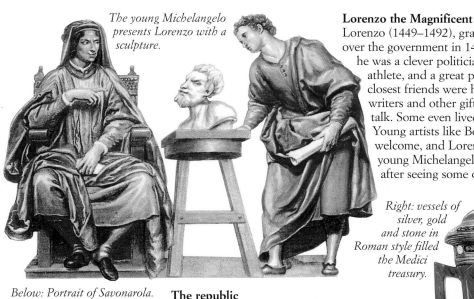

The young Michelangelo presents Lorenzo with a sculpture.

Lorenzo the Magnificent

Lorenzo (1449–1492), grandson of Cosimo the Elder, took over the government in 1469, at age 20. Like all the Medici, he was a clever politician, but he was also a poet, athlete, and a great patron of artists and writers. His closest friends were humanist scholars. At his palace, writers and other gifted people gathered for learned talk. Some even lived there rent-free. Young artists like Botticelli found a welcome, and Lorenzo invited the young Michelangelo to live there after seeing some of his work.

Right: vessels of silver, gold and stone in Roman style filled the Medici treasury.

Above: Arms of the Pazzi. Left: A medallion commemorating the death of Giuliano de' Medici in the Pazzi plot.

The republic

Florence was the home of liberal humanism, but it had another side. Savonarola (1452–1498) was a puritanical friar who denounced corrupt rulers and clergy and, by his powerful sermons, inspired ordinary people. In the troubles following the French invasion of Italy in 1494, the Medici were driven from Florence. Savonarola took over, hoping to make Florence a city of God. He set up an honest, democratic, and severely religious government. But he had powerful enemies, including the Pope, and eventually the Florentines. In 1510 a Spanish army restored the Medici.

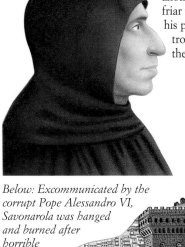

Below: Portrait of Savonarola.

Below: Excommunicated by the corrupt Pope Alessandro VI, Savonarola was hanged and burned after horrible tortures.

The Pazzi conspiracy

Lorenzo the Magnificent wisely and skillfully kept Florence out of war. But his most dangerous enemies were at home–the Pazzi family. With the Pope's support, the Pazzi planned to murder Lorenzo and his brother, Giuliano, at Easter, in 1478. During mass in the cathedral, the Pazzi attacked with knives. Giuliano was killed but Lorenzo, though stabbed in the neck, escaped. He took fierce revenge. He and his supporters killed about 250 relatives and friends of the Pazzi.

The Medici outside Italy

The Medici became a prominent European dynasty, linked by marriage with many royal families. The two main branches of the family were descended from Cosimo the Elder and his brother, Lorenzo. Cosimo's descendants were rulers of Florence, and Lorenzo's became grand dukes of Tuscany. The Medici also provided: two queens of France, Catherine de Médicis and Marie de Médicis; four popes, Leo X, Clement VII, Pius IV, and Leo XI, and two ruling dukes.

Above: The Pope blesses Catherine de Médicis as she marries the future king of France.

Left: This magnificent casket was Clement VII's wedding present to the future Henri II of France and Catherine, Clement's niece, in 1533.

The siege of 1530

In 1527 the Medici were again expelled from Florence and a republic was established. But Florence, torn by rivalries, no longer controlled its own fate. The big powers, Spain and France, decided things in Italy. By agreement with Pope Clement VII, who was a Medici, the republic was besieged by the forces of the Emperor Charles V (who was also king of Spain). With people starving, Florence was forced to surrender, and Medici rule was restored.

Grand Duchy of Tuscany in 1574 ☐

- **Massa**
- **Lucca**
- **Florence**
- **Volterra**
- **Siena**

☐ *Principality of Massa*
☐ *Stato dei Presidi*
☐ *Principality of Piombino*
☐ *State of Siena*
☐ *Republic of Lucca*

This map shows Tuscany in the 16th century.

Right: Cosimo I (1519–1574), first grand duke of Tuscany, with his family.

The Grand Duchy

Thanks to the alliance of Pope and Emperor, Alessandro de' Medici became head of the republic in 1531. Within a year, the signory (city government) was abolished, Alessandro was created governor for life, and his power became hereditary. The golden age of Florence was over and it became the capital of the Grand Duchy of Tuscany. The Medici family continued to rule as grand dukes until 1737, when the title passed to another family.

Art of the Early Renaissance

The rediscovery of Classical civilization in the early Renaissance encouraged people to take more interest in themselves as individuals and in the world around them. This, and their admiration for the realistic art of ancient Rome, led to new subjects for painters and sculptors. The main subjects of medieval art had been religious. Now, artists adopted other themes, from Classical mythology or, in the Netherlands especially, everyday life. Newly inspired, artists developed new techniques and ways of making pictures, and their work became admired for its individual qualities. Artists respected Classical art not only as a model but also because it revealed what worked and what did not. They realized that creating art required serious study; theory was as important as skill with a paintbrush or chisel.

Below: A detail from a fresco by Masaccio. Apart from the halo, these look like real people.

A medallion (about 1450) bearing the head of Alberti.

Alberti

Leon Baptista Alberti (1404–1472) was a Florentine humanist. He was also an architect and probably a painter and sculptor too, but his importance in art comes from his writings. His book on painting was the first important work on the artistic theories of the Renaissance. Among many other things, Alberti gave the first explanation of perspective and discussed the new subject of history painting, which at that time meant chiefly Classical history and mythology.

Below: The great German artist Albrecht Dürer (1471–1528) demonstrates a device for determining perspective.

Masaccio

Though he died at only 27 (in 1428) Masaccio (a nickname) is recognized as the first of the great 15th century painters in northern Italy. At a time when most artists were still working in the International Gothic style, he painted fully realistic human figures to scale in recognizable spaces and employed the technique of chiaroscuro (light and shade) to give them three-dimensional solidity.

Left: An exercise of perspective in a painting by Fra Filippo Lippi.

Perspective

An object has three dimensions (height, width, and depth) but a picture has only two. Perspective is a system of showing depth on a two-dimensional surface. It was invented in Florence in the early 15th century, and it depends on an illusion. Parallel lines, which in reality never meet, draw closer together in the picture as distance increases. Some artists were so delighted with this that they chose subjects specially to show off their command of perspective (see above).

Right: Detail of a female figure, a symbol of the richness of nature, from a drawing by Botticelli.

The 15th century achievement

By 1500 the startling advances of the Renaissance style were generally accepted. The way was prepared for the High Renaissance (about 1500 to 1530), when the great painters and sculptors seemed to have perfect command of their art. Although the early Renaissance was far more than a period of preparation in some ways it fell short of the perfection of the High Renaissance. Human figures and feelings often seem stylized rather than real, and parts of a picture are often better than the whole.

Early Renaissance painters

In the 15th century artists believed that successful work came from hard study, observation, and investigation. Faced with the difficulty of presenting a three-dimensional space on a flat canvas, or calculating the effects of light and color, they looked for a system; they believed that there were rules that governed these things. Yet, while they studied nature closely so as to represent it realistically, they actually introduced something extra. Like their Classical forbears, they gave their subjects a certain ideal quality, a beauty or significance, which a bluntly realistic picture would not have done.

Donatello

One of the most individual and influential artists of the early Renaissance was the sculptor Donatello. Like many others, he traveled to Rome to examine Classical remains (there was, of course, much more Roman sculpture surviving than painting). The effect on his style can be seen by comparing his St. George (page 9), which has a beyond-this-world, medieval air, and his bronze David (right), done after his visit to Rome.

Left: Donatello's David *is both a celebration of the human form and a realistic, ragamuffin shepherd boy.*

The minor arts

Many Renaissance painters were trained as goldsmiths, and the distinction between what we call the fine arts and the work of craftsmen, though increasing, was less defined than in later times. Besides the sculpture of artists like Donatello, there were more modest, popular art forms, like that of the Della Robbia family, who made beautiful colored and glazed plaques in terra-cotta (see page 9). There was also the costly, intricate work of the goldsmiths, which carried on a great medieval tradition.

Left: An altar with gold and precious stones, an example of the rich and intricate work of the goldsmiths.

Left: Virgin and child (about 1500) in tin-glazed earthenware.

Below: Dated as early as 1425, Campin's triptych is painted in the new medium of oil.

Below: This painting by Fra Angelico (1443) shows the medieval (Gothic) spirit still flourishing in 15th century Florence.

Altarpieces

Among the finest examples of 15th century religious art were altarpieces, pictures that stood on or behind the altar of a church, usually in the form of a triptych (three panels). This illustration (right) shows a side panel from a triptych by the Flemish artist, Robert Campin. The figure is Joseph, husband of Mary, who was a carpenter. As was the custom, clothes, tools, and buildings belong to 15th century Europe, not 1st century Palestine.

Left: A portrait of van Eyck (died 1441), the greatest Flemish painter of his day, who helped to perfect the technique of oil painting.

Oil paint

The great works of Italian 15th century painters are mainly frescoes, pictures on walls (or ceilings) that were painted a section at a time on wet plaster with watercolor. For easel paintings on wood or canvas, a richer, more versatile medium was invented, oil paint. Though a kind of oil paint had been used for houses in ancient times, the technique was probably developed in the Netherlands, and brought to Italy by visiting Flemish painters during the 15th century.

Religious art

Although Renaissance artists adopted a much greater range of subject-matter, religious pictures still formed much the largest category. Practically every Italian painter painted a Madonna and Child (Mary and Jesus), often many of them. The Church liked pictures, which often made a greater impact than sermons on the congregation. Also the greatest single patron of Renaissance artists was the Pope.

Portraits

Portraits, in paint or marble, were not new, although realistic portraits were rare in Europe before the 14th century. Besides rulers, bishops, and other dignitaries, wealthy patrons often wanted their portrait painted. Before Henry VIII of England agreed to marry an unseen German princess, he sent his court painter to make a portrait of her. Like most official portraits, it was flattering. Painters had to remember who their sitter was, not just present an honest likeness.

Right: Portrait of a lady, by Fra Filippo Lippi, about 1440, when the fashionable view was from the side.

Tombs

Clear boundaries can never be drawn between changing styles in art. Early Renaissance artists in Italy did not suddenly turn into copiers of Roman art. Sculptors like Donatello or Jacopo della Quercia adapted the ancient style in their own way. This tomb (right) by Jacopo, shows evidence of both Classical influence (the fat little cherubs for instance) and a medieval heritage.

Below: Tomb of a lady (1406), in Lucca Cathedral, by Jacopo della Quercia, who was later an influence on Michelangelo.

Early Renaissance Architecture

Ordinary people might never see the frescoes of Raphael in the Vatican, but they could not help seeing the great church of St Peter's. Architecture was the most public of the arts. For that reason, it was the best way for people to express pride in their city. Much of the great wealth of a city such as Florence was spent on splendid buildings. When it came to designing their new buildings, Italians naturally looked back to their own cultural roots. The Gothic style that swept over most of Europe in the Middle Ages had never really caught on in Italy. Many ancient Roman buildings still stood, and although Italians did build some Gothic buildings (Milan cathedral being one), other medieval buildings were Romanesque, a style that also derived from ancient Rome.

Above: Brunelleschi presents his plans for the Medici church of St. Lorenzo to Cosimo de' Medici (1418).

Above: Brunelleschi designed hoists to lift brick and stone (and the workmen's lunch) over 160 feet (50 m) to the dome.

Brunelleschi

Brunelleschi is seen as the first true Renaissance architect. He was the first master architect, who controlled the whole project from design to construction. He trained as a goldsmith and sculptor, but he was an intellectual who understood engineering principles such as stress and knew the calculation governing the curve of pointed arches. This calculation was known to Gothic builders but not to ancient Rome. His style was not particularly antique, except in the decorative details.

The dome of Florence

Brunelleschi won a competition to build the dome of Florence cathedral in 1418. He promised to do it without centering the huge wooden scaffolding used in roofing large spaces. People said the task was impossible. Brunelleschi had in mind the Pantheon in Rome (128 A.D.), but his dome, mainly brick, is eight-sided (not round), much steeper (to help support its own weight), and is actually two domes, one inside the other.

Left: Brunelleschi's dome, owed more to Gothic than Classical architecture.

Above: The Pazzi chapel, Brunelleschi's last building, was designed on a system of circles inside squares.

Brunelleschi's proportions

The design of the cathedral dome was the result of construction problems. Perhaps Brunelleschi would have preferred a round dome, but it had to be eight-sided because the eight-sided drum already existed. His principles of proportion, based on mathematics, were better seen in the sacristy of St. Lorenzo. This church is square in plan, with its walls the same height as the sides of the square, so the building forms a perfect cube.

Left: The sign of the masons and wood-carvers guild of Florence.

Stone masons

The masons who constructed the cathedral were a strongly united craft. In northern Europe they moved from site to site, living in their own lodges for months or years at a time and forming a brotherhood apart from the rest of society. The master mason was the man in charge of the building until the rise of the architect reduced him to a kind of consultant-foreman. As skilled craftsmen, however, masons played a vital part in the building boom of the 15th century.

Right: The high-quality marble found in Italian quarries was used for the visible parts of fine buildings and for sculpture.

Roman remains

In 15th century Rome, Classical buildings and sculpture, in various states of repair, could be seen everywhere. They were so common that people used the ancient stone for new buildings. Florentine artists like Brunelleschi and Donatello visited Rome to study ancient techniques. Architects learned to use all the decorative elements of ancient architecture (such as columns), but did not at first fully understand its principles.

Below: Vitruvius was half forgotten until Poggio Bracciolini drew attention to a copy at the abbey of Saint Gall in 1414.

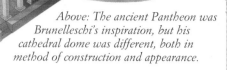

Above: The ancient Pantheon was Brunelleschi's inspiration, but his cathedral dome was different, both in method of construction and appearance.

Alberti's church of Santa Maria Novella, Florence, was based on a complex geometrical system believed to be related to music.

Vitruvius

Vitruvius, who lived in the 1st century B.C., was the author of the only surviving ancient work on architecture. He became hugely important to 15th-century people eager to recapture the greatness of ancient Rome. His *De architectura* is a rather difficult book to read and strictly practical. While he calls for harmony, good proportions, dignity, and strength, his work reduces architecture to a set of strict rules.

A Classical vocabulary

Brunelleschi's Ospedale degli Innocenti (see page 8), often called the first Renaissance building, uses a Classical vocabulary, of Corinthian columns, round arches, etc., yet is not like any ancient Roman building. Later architects followed Roman rules, but Renaissance buildings were never just copies. Their purpose was different. The 15th century wanted churches, public buildings, and large palaces; not temples, amphitheaters, and public baths.

Alberti

The Renaissance produced its own Vitruvius in Leon Battista Alberti, author (1452) of *De re aedificatoria* (*About Building Matters*). He discusses proportion, the Classical orders, and town planning, but is far less strict and teacher-like than Vitruvius. Alberti said the beauty of a building lies in the harmony of all the parts, which should be done in such a way that anything added, or taken away, could only change it for the worse.

Left: Alberti's large church of St. Andrea in Mantua is based on a Roman triumphal arch—a large arch flanked by two smaller ones.

Right: The figure of the saint in Mantegna's picture suggests that he had studied antique statues as well as buildings.

The ideal city

Alberti discussed town planning in his famous book, and the notion of a perfect city appealed strongly to many artists. Medieval cities were dark and crowded with narrow streets. The ideal city was open and spacious but also, it often appeared, uninhabited. Few new towns were built, so there was little opportunity to put Alberti's ideas for large-scale town planning in practice. The schemes of the artists were really exercises in geometry and perspective.

Left: Plan for Palmanova, a rare new town was designed by Giovanni Savorgnano with defense in mind. It was also beautifully symmetrical.

Below: An ideal, city painted probably by Piero della Francesca about 1450, significantly empty of people.

Architecture in art

The main subject of 15th century Italian art was the human figure. Though painters were generally less interested in landscape, features of Classical art and architecture naturally found their way into pictures. The loving care that Mantegna lavished on architectural fragments in his St. Sebastian (1470) shows his longing to recapture the glorious, Classical past.

Rome and the Papacy

After the Medici were banished from Florence in 1494, many artists moved to Rome, which replaced Florence as the heart of the Renaissance. Rome had once been the capital of a huge empire, and a world center of government, knowledge, and art. Later it became the headquarters of the Christian Church and residence of the papacy. It remained, in a sense, the capital of Europe. Rome, with its grand marble buildings, was called the Eternal City when London and Paris were still small wooden towns. Bad times came in the 14th century when the pope was forced into exile in France. Rome lacked a proper government and fell into ruin. Things improved when the Great Schism ended (1443), and the pope returned. In less than 100 years, it was again the greatest, and certainly the wealthiest, city in Europe. That revival was chiefly due to the Renaissance popes.

Return of the papacy
The papacy recovered some of its lost prestige when it returned to Rome. Everyone rallied round Nicholas V after rival popes had disappeared. But most popes over the next century failed to live up to their task. They talked of two great aims: at home, reform of the Church; abroad, a crusade against the Ottoman Turks. They talked but did not act. Even an intelligent and well-meaning pope like Pius II (1458–1464) decided, in the end, not to stir up trouble and so nothing happened.

Left: Figure from the tomb of John XXIII, one of three rival popes during the Great Schism.

Detail from one of Raphael's frescoes, the Fire in the Borgo, *in the Vatican. It was commissioned by Leo X, a Medici pope.*

Renaissance popes
Most Renaissance popes came from powerful Italian families. They were princes first and priests second. Many, like Leo X, a Medici, understood politics and governed skillfully. Julius II was more comfortable in a soldier's helmet than a bishop's miter. The Renaissance popes wanted power and wealth for themselves and their families, and they knew how to get it. In any case, the papacy enjoyed a large income, as every town in Europe paid dues to the pope.

Above: A map of Rome in about 1470.

Papal patronage
Nicholas V, the first Renaissance pope, besides founding the Vatican Library, planned to pull down the old basilica of St. Peter's to build a grand new church in the spirit of the age. Whatever their failings, the Renaissance popes were cultured men, devoted to the arts. Most of them contributed to the adornment of Rome and hired the finest artists including Raphael, Michelangelo, and Leonardo to carry out their ambitious plans.

Left: A detail of one of Fra Angelico's frescoes in the chapel of Nicholas V.

Rome transformed
In Renaissance times a ruler had to display his power. The Renaissance popes spared no expense to beautify their capital with grand buildings and works of art.

Right: Sixtus IV (pope 1471–1484) began building the Sistine Chapel in the Vatican.

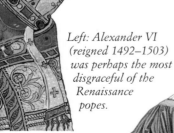

- **Ferrara**
- **Ravenna**
- **Urbino**
- **Spoleto** • **Ascoli**
- **Orvieto** •
- **Viterbo**
- **Rome**

Papal States
areas under their control

Papal States in 1513.

Left: Alexander VI (reigned 1492–1503) was perhaps the most disgraceful of the Renaissance popes.

The Borgia
The worst popes, whom the Dutch humanist Erasmus called the scourge of the human race, were Sixtus IV and Innocent VIII, both violent, cruel, and greedy men. Alexander VI (Rodrigo de Borgia), the worst, was able, intelligent, and energetic, but also totally ruthless. His son, Cesare Borgia, was an ambitious prince who showed no mercy to anyone in his quest to make the Romagna (major part of the Papal States) his private domain.

Right: Cesare Borgia (1475–1507) was the model for the unscrupulous ruler in Machiavelli's The Prince.

TIMELINE OF POPES

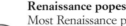

| Nicholas V | Callistus III | Pius II | Paul II | Sixtus IV | Innocent VIII | Alexander VI | Pius III | Julius II | Leo X | Hadrian VI | Clement VII | Paul III | Julius III | Marcellus II | Paul IV | Pius IV | Pius V | Gregory XIII | Sixtus V | Urban VII | Gregory XIV | Innocent IX | Clement VIII |

1450　　　　　　　　　　1500　　　　　　　　　　1550　　　　　　　　　　1600

Below: Michelangelo's Pietà *(the Virgin Mary with the body of Jesus) in St. Peter's.*

Right: A medallion made to commemorate the founding of the new St Peter's in 1506.

St. Peter's

The plan to replace St Peter's, the chief church of Western Christianity, had been discussed for years, but it was not until 1506 that the old church was finally torn down. The architect Bramante, who had recently built the Tempietto, the first true Renaissance building in Rome, prepared designs for a new St Peter's. Directed by a succession of great artists (including Michelangelo), the church was finished a century later.

Julius II

Julius II was 60 when elected pope and was not expected to live for ten years, though he did (1503–1513). Like many other Renaissance popes, he was hardly fit to be a priest, let alone the spiritual leader of Europe, but he was the greatest of the papal patrons. He hired Michelangelo and Raphael as fresco-painters and let them choose their own subjects. He put Bramante in charge of a vast building program.

Right: Bramante's Tempietto *(1502) was inspired by round temples in ancient Rome.*

Below: A figure from one of Raphael's frescoes in the Vatican palace, said to be a portrait of Michelangelo.

The Swiss guard

The Swiss Guard was a band of Swiss mercenaries first hired as a papal bodyguard by Julius II. Its members came from the cantons of Lucerne and Zurich, in Switzerland, and their uniform is said to have been designed by Michelangelo. They still exist, though now there are only about 100 of them, and they still wear the 16th-century style uniform, but now perform ceremonial duties only.

Pigna courtyard

Belvedere courtyard

Borgia Tower

Sistine chapel

St. Peter's

A member of the Swiss guard.

The obelisk

St. Peter's Square, laid out by Bernini in the 17th century

Left: A Hellenistic sculpture discovered in Rome in 1506. Such works influenced contemporary artists.

Below: The new generation of artists are sometimes called Mannerists. This is a detail from a painting by Giuliano Romano, one of the best of them.

Artists in Rome

The High Renaissance style lasted only a short time and was created by a few artists of genius, who shared the same influences and had similar aims. But a remarkable feature of the art of that time was its diversity. Although they had so much in common, artists like Raphael and Michelangelo, for example, are quite different in style. Yet each artist benefited, if in different ways, from the influence of others working in the same city at the same time.

The Sack of Rome

During the 1520s Emperor Charles V of Spain, had an army in northern Italy. He was on bad terms with the Pope, Clement VII. Many in his army were Germans and followers of the Protestant reformer, Luther. They had not been paid for weeks. In 1527 they ran out of control and attacked Rome, an evil city in their eyes. The destruction lasted for weeks. Blood ran with wine in the gutters, black smoke rose from burning buildings. This event destroyed Renaissance Rome.

Below: Rioting soldiers attack Castel Sant'Angelo, where the pope was prisoner.

A new style

The Sack of Rome marked the end of an age as artists fled the city. In the final phase of the Italian Renaissance, the leading city would be Venice. However, within a few years, popes were again active as patrons in Rome and a new generation of artists appeared. They were as talented as their predecessors and had learned all their skills, but the style had changed. While their ability is obvious, these artists seemed to be showing off.

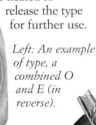

Chinese printing: The plate is assembled, ink brushed on, paper applied and rubbed, then peeled away.

The Printing Revolution

Of all the developments that made the Renaissance possible, the most important was the invention of printing with movable, metal type. In 1450, all books were copied by hand. To produce one copy of a book could take many months. The printing press made it possible to produce hundreds of copies in a few days. Moreover, the copies were identical. Each word was exactly the same wherever it occurred, abolishing all the variations (and mistakes) of manuscript (handwriting). Manuscript books were luxury items, which few people could afford. Printed books were far cheaper, and so became more widely available. That had huge effects on history. Without printing, Luther's books would have been unknown to all but a tiny handful of people and the Protestant Reformation may never have occurred.

Above: Gutenberg with a copy of his first printed Bible.

China

The Chinese had discovered printing 1,000 years before Gutenberg. They had already invented paper and suitable ink. The Chinese characters to be printed were carved, in relief, on wood blocks. Ink was applied to the characters with a brush, a sheet of paper laid on the block and rubbed down, to transfer the image from wood to paper. In the 11th century, a Chinese printer developed movable, reusable type, made of a mixture of glue, wax, and ash, hardened by heating. After printing, the plate was heated to release the type for further use.

Left: An example of type, a combined O and E (in reverse).

Type

To make type, a letter was first carved in relief in a steel punch and driven into a softer piece of metal (the matrix) to make an impression of the letter. Lead alloy was melted and poured into this mold. When cool, it produced an impression of the letter in reverse, which appeared the right way when printed. Thousands of letters could be produced from the same mold (coins were already made in this way). The type was arranged in trays. The typesetter selected type from the trays and fitted it on to his stick, to build up words and a whole line. The line of type was then placed in a tray called a galley. The typesetter prepared the next line, and so on until he had completed a page.

Early printers were also publishers and often book-sellers. Above: The famous colophon of the Aldine Press, anchor and dolphin.

The Aldine Press

Gutenberg went bankrupt and lost his business, but others were more successful. Aldus Manutius (1449–1515), who had studied with the humanist scholar Pico della Mirandola, set up his Aldine Press in Venice in 1490. He published classical Greek texts for the first time, as well as writing from Petrarch and others, employing the best scholars as editors. His books were small, pocket-size, inexpensive, and beautifully printed. Among other innovations of the Aldine Press was italic type.

Above: Map showing major centers of printing in Renaissance Europe. Though it began in Germany, Italy soon took the lead.

Left: Printers tried to make their books look like manuscripts. Gutenberg's type followed the Gothic style of northern Europe. Italian printers adopted the easier-to-read Carolingian script.

Gutenberg

Printing in Europe was a German invention. Many craftsmen experimented with printing methods from the early 15th century, but the man who produced the first printed book, a Latin Bible, was Johannes Gutenberg of Mainz, in 1455. Gutenberg first had to discover a way to produce the metal type and assemble it to make up a whole page. The second problem was to invent a printing press to transfer the inked page of type to paper and to turn out many copies quickly. He solved these problems by adopting the principle of the screw press, which was used for crushing grapes or olives.

Below: A page from Gutenberg's Bible. People were amazed by its clarity. Nearly 50 copies still survive.

The spread of knowledge

The dramatic effect of the mass production of books is proved by the speed at which printing spread and the number of books that were published. Religious books were most numerous, followed by works of the ancient Greeks and Romans. The first encyclopedia appeared in 1460, and the first Bible (in German) a few years later. Stories for pure entertainment were coming off the presses within 50 years.

When books became widely available, more people learned to read. By 1500 most women above the peasant class could read.

Printing trades

Gutenberg probably had to do most things himself, including casting his own type. But printing, like other crafts, soon developed several different trades, each with its own independent guild. They included bookbinders, who were sometimes also booksellers. When the printed sheets arrived in the bindery from the printer, they were folded, cut, and sewn together between strong leather-covered boards to make a book. This was an old trade; the most beautiful and costly bindings were made in monasteries in the late Middle Ages. With the huge expansion of book production, bindings became cheaper and plainer.

Left: A bookbinder at work.

Paper

The spread of printing depended on a large supply of paper. Medieval scribes wrote on vellum or parchment, scraped animal skin. For large-scale book production, these materials were too expensive. Paper, made from fibrous material such as cloth or wood, reached Europe from China via Muslim Spain about 1150. From the 13th century, water-driven paper mills in Italy produced growing quantities of paper. The fibrous material was pulped, a screen was dipped into it and removed with a thin layer of pulp. As it was dried and pressed, the fibers fused together to form a sheet of paper.

A boy carries away finished sheets in a 16th century paper mill (the screw press can be seen in the background, and the mill wheels through the window).

The printer's shop

When the typesetter completed a page of type, it was placed on the stone bed of the press, inked, and paper was laid over it. A flat plate was lowered and pressed hard on the paper by the screw, turned by a handle. Then it was released, the printed page removed, and the next sheet put in place. Both sides of the paper could be printed (impossible in the Chinese system). Minor problems, such as smudged ink and uneven impressions, had to be overcome, but the basic technology of the printing press was not a problem for the skilled craftsmen of the 15th century.

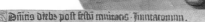

Illustrations

The technique of printing from engraved wooden blocks (woodcuts) was well-known. It was used for printing patterns on cloth and, from about 1400, paper. Renaissance artists like Mantegna and Dürer were skilled in wood engraving, the chief way to print pictures. Color could be added by hand or by repeat printing with different colors. The old tradition of decorative first letters continued in printed books. Sometimes they were painted additions, but the Mainz Psalter (1457) of the Gutenberg press, was printed in three colors in one impression—black (letterpress), red, and blue (initial letters).

The method of printing an initial letter in the Mainz Psalter: The type consists of two interlinked sections, one that prints the letter, the other the decoration. They had to be inked separately.

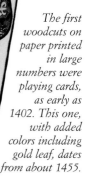

The first woodcuts on paper printed in large numbers were playing cards, as early as 1402. This one, with added colors including gold leaf, dates from about 1455.

Above: The sons of Federico Gonzaga, detail of a painting by Mantegna.

Mantua

Mantua was a small state and rather poor. It survived because it was defended by lakes and marshes. Its rulers, the Gonzaga, were good generals and had useful links to German princes and, by marriage, to the Este and Montefeltro families. Alberti spent his last years in Mantua, and the great Mantegna was court painter. Mantegna's association with the Gonzaga is an example of the wonderful works resulting from the combination of gifted artist and intelligent patron.

Left: Medal struck to commemorate a victory of Giovanni Francesco Gonzaga (died 1444), general of the Holy Roman emperor.

Northern Italy

In later years, Italians looked back to the late 15th century as a golden age. The 40 years before the French invasion of 1494 were fairly peaceful and very prosperous. Opportunities existed for anyone with talent, and fortunes could be made. Life in the independent, princely courts was exciting, comfortable, and highly civilized. Rulers like the Gonzaga in Mantua used the profits from their careers as condottieri (mercenary generals) to build magnificent palaces and create centers of learning. Italy had one weakness though. It was divided. The main states were Florence, Milan, Venice, the Papacy, and Naples; none of which were very large and each with its own weaknesses. The many smaller states were still independent, usually ruled by a dominant family, but with the support of the people. Outside Italy were much larger powers. Ambitious foreign rulers saw Italy as a treasure house: very rich, but in military terms, very weak.

Left: Gold coin of Galeazzo Maria Sforza, who introduced rice growing. He was murdered in 1476.

Above: A figure, perhaps Music, by the Ferrarese court painter Cosimo Tura, whose style was part medieval, part Classical, but mostly personal.

Milan

The Visconti dukes of Milan created a strong and stable state. Agriculture was highly advanced and, as a military power, Milan was about the strongest in Italy. With the people's approval, the Sforza family took over in 1450. Other Italian states saw the value of a strong state in the north as defense against invaders, and made alliances with the Sforza. The duchy continued to prosper under Sforza rule.

Below: Galeazzo Maria Sforza, second Sforza duke of Milan, in a portrait by Pollaiuolo.

DUCHY OF SAVOY
MONTFERRAT
Milan •
DUCHY OF MILAN
Genoa •
REPUBLIC OF GENOA
REPUBLIC OF VENICE
• Venice
• Mantua
• Ferrara
Bologna •
• Faenza
REPUBLIC OF FLORENCE
• Urbino
REPUBLIC OF SIENA
PAPAL STATES
Rome •
KINGDOM OF NAPLES

The Este of Ferrara

The Este were an old noble family from the town of Ferrara (they also held Modena). They were well-educated, and very popular. Ferrara was within the Papal States and both the pope and Venice had designs on it, but it kept its independence thanks to its allies, especially Milan. The Este represented the finest society of the early Renaissance, in which the tradition of medieval chivalry mingled with Classical culture.

Left: Map showing Italy in 1492. The sovereignty of the Emperor meant little, but in the Papal States popes tried to enforce their control.

Below: Fresco from the Palazzo Schifanoia, in Ferrara, with a Classical theme. It shows Venus with mars kneeling before her.

Left: Gold coin of Giovanni II Bentivoglio (1443–1508), last of his family to rule Bologna.

Bologna

The site of Europe's first university, Bologna became a commune in the 12th century. In the 15th century, the city, which lay in the Papal States, was held by the Visconti, then by the descendants of an earlier ruler named Giovanni Bentivoglio. Like most Renaissance princes, they were keen patrons of the arts, but when, following Cesare Borgia's campaigns, Pope Julius II set out to impose papal rule on the cities of the Romagna, the Bentivogli were driven out.

Venice

Citizens of Venice believed they lived in the greatest state the world had seen since ancient Rome. The nobles controlled government, but all classes were well treated, taxes were light, and laws fair. Venice increased its possessions in Italy, partly as compensation for its shrinking influence in the East after the Turks captured Constantinople (1453). But, Venice expanded in Italy at the expense of other states, and so made enemies.

Left: Portrait of the Doge (Leader) by the Venetian master Bellini. Real power belonged to a small council of nobles.

Urbino

Urbino, birthplace of Raphael, was a small city perched on a hill. It was one of the finest centers of Renaissance art and literature. Its reputation was largely due to Duke Federico de Montefeltro (reigned 1444–1482), a perfect Renaissance prince, whose family had ruled since the 12th century. He converted the castle into a beautiful palace and his court, if less glamorous than Florence or Ferrara, was intellectually just as lively.

Right: Federico was both soldier and scholar.

The city of Venice

Venice was nearing the end of its greatest period and about to lose control of the spice trade that made it rich. But in 1494, it was still a city of splendid buildings and rich entertainment. After Florence, it was the queen of Renaissance cities. In spite of secret police, Venice had a free, easy-going air that attracted artists, and its buildings showed a stimulating mixture of influences–Gothic, Classical, and Byzantine.

Left: A 15th-century view of St. Mark's Square, Venice, with the Doge's Palace at top right.

Left: Another resident of Urbino was Baldassare Castiglione (1478–1529), diplomat and writer. His book The Courtier was, like Machiavelli's The Prince, famous throughout Europe.

State painters

Most rulers employed official artists more or less full time. The Venetian Titian was court painter to the Emperor Charles V. Once, when Titian was painting Charles' portrait, he dropped his brush. The Emperor bent down and picked it up for him. That gesture of respect showed the high status that a great artist enjoyed during the Renaissance.

Detail from a painting by the Venetian master, Titian (1488–1576).

Genoa

Genoa, once the rival of Venice in sea-borne trade, suffered from the advances of the Ottoman Turks, who took over all its trading posts on the Black Sea. Its Mediterranean colonies were also lost. Under Milanese and later French rule, the gap between the wealthy upper class and ordinary citizens grew, causing conflicts. But, in 1528, Andrea Doria, head of Genoa's greatest family, threw off French rule and restored stable government.

Above: The Doria Palace. Genoa's many palaces were built by merchants who profited from Spanish-American trade.

Left: This elegant sculpture from about 1500 shows the influence of ancient Rome on Tullio Lombardo, one of a family of famous sculptors who worked in Venice.

Minor Arts

In spite of the status of a painter such as Titian, the arts and crafts were not yet specialized, and those who practiced what we would call the fine arts also produced what we might call craft work. All the decorative arts flourished. The town of Faenza, near Bologna, produced large amounts of colored glazed pottery (the recipe came from Muslim Spain). In France it is still called faïence, though in Italy it is called maiolica, after Majorca, the center of Spanish-Italian trade.

Right: Dish from Faenza showing the Three Graces, a Classical subject.

The French invasion

The Italian golden age came to an end when Charles VIII of France invaded in 1494. He came to assert a French claim to the throne of Naples, but that was just an excuse. Within a few weeks he held not only Naples but Milan, Florence, and Rome as well. He soon lost them again, but the damage was done. Italy lost control of its own affairs: It became the prize for which foreign dynasties like the Valois (French) and Habsburg (German and, later, Spanish) competed.

Left: Charles VIII's dreams of glory came to nothing, and he died in 1498 at the age of 27.

Spain and Portugal

The late 15th century was a dramatic period in the Iberian peninsula. The most important event was the union of the crowns of Aragon and Castile, the largest kingdoms. With the later conquest of Navarre, Spain became united under one ruler, though the different parts still kept their own governments, and Portugal remained independent. In 1492 the last Muslim state, Granada, was conquered, ending 800 years of war between Christians and Muslims. All Jews were expelled from the country, and a Spanish expedition, led by Columbus, discovered the New World. Just a few years later, in 1498, the Portuguese discovered a route to India. These events affected the course of history far beyond the Iberian peninsula.

Carved figures of Ferdinand and Isabella, whom the Pope called "the Catholic kings."

Ferdinand and Isabella

In 1469, Ferdinand of Aragon married Isabella, the future queen of Castile, which was the largest Spanish kingdom with about 5 million people (nearly 20 times as many as Aragon). Both monarchs were able politicians. They inherited a chaotic medieval country, but by Ferdinand's death in 1516 (Isabella died in 1504), they had built the foundations of a stable Renaissance state, soon to be the richest and most powerful in Europe.

Spain in the late 15th century

Spain's chief weakness was economic. Although most people worked in farming and stock raising, Castile did not grow enough food for its population. The wool trade favored by government was more profitable, but not for the peasants, who were hungry and rebellious. The departure of Jewish merchants persecuted by the Spanish Inquisition was a serious blow to commerce.

Above: A synagogue in 14th-century Spain, whose large Jewish minority had prospered under Muslim rule.

Detail from an altar screen, a gift of Don López de Mendoza, marquis of Santillana (1398–1458), patron and poet, who wrote sonnets in the manner of Petrarch.

St. John's Church, in Toledo, was built under Isabella. While Bramante was planning the Tempietto in Rome, Spain preferred its own late-Gothic Style for churches.

Humanism in Spain

Humanism made its mark in Spain, especially Castile, quite early. Lectures on the Latin poets were given at the University of Salamanca as early as 1473. Humanist interests were also strong at the court of Ferdinand and Isabella and, even more, in the new university at Alcalá de Henares (founded 1508). The leading Spanish humanist scholar, Antonio de Nebrija, went to teach there and it became a center of Greek studies, producing a new version of the New Testament in 1514.

Church and state

The Catholic Kings enjoyed unusual control over the Church, especially in the American colonies where they appointed bishops and received tithes, the taxes normally paid to the Church. The Spanish Inquisition, founded 1478, (like the medieval Inquisition) was not a papal court to try heretics. It was a government weapon against *conversos* (Jews turned Christian), who often held important positions in Spain. Its savage operations led to the expulsion of all Jews in 1492.

Below: Universities in Renaissance Spain and Portugal.

Valladolid

Salamanca • • Sigüenza

• Alcalá de Henares

Coimbra

Valencia •

• Ubeda

Baeza •

The Italian influence

All the early humanists in Spain were either Italians or graduates of Italian universities (the Spanish humanist Nebrija had spent ten years in Italy). In the fine arts, flourishing under royal patronage, Italian influence was less.

Below: Detail from a painting by the Spanish artist Pedro Berruguete, about 1500. It shows that he had spent some time at the Italian court of Urbino.

Valencia

Once an independent Muslim kingdom, Valencia kept some independence under Aragon, with its own royal governor. Muslim influence remained strong (the dialect still contains Arabic words) in this civilized region. Valencia had the first Spanish printing press (1474) and its own distinctive school of painting.

Muslim-Spanish vase. A thin metal film on the pottery gives it a shimmering effect.

Madonna and Child, *marble relief by Diego de Siloé, who had studied in Italy.*

Right: The 17-year-old Charles V, future sovereign of the Netherlands, Germany, half of Italy, Spain, bits of eastern France and North Africa, and a growing American empire.

Below: The double-headed imperial eagle and coat of arms of Charles V.

Charles V

Carlos I (his Spanish name) had never been to Spain until he inherited Ferdinand's crown in 1516. In 1519 he succeeded his Habsburg father as the Emperor Karl V. His personal empire was huge, and so were his problems. His lands were not united; he was not an absolute ruler anywhere; he was always in debt; the Turks threatened the Habsburg heartland; and the Reformation shattered religious unity. Worn out, Charles abdicated in 1556, dividing his lands between his brother and son.

Right: Bust of Philip II. Unlike his father, he never left Spain. His intolerant indirect government made him unpopular in his other dominions.

Philip II

The reign of Philip II (1556–1598) and his father, Charles V, coincided with the Golden Age of Spain, when literature and the arts flourished as never before. Due largely to American treasure, Spain became the richest country in Europe. Though he was not Holy Roman Emperor, Philip also inherited his father's costly and difficult role of chief defender of the Roman Catholic Church.

Royal patronage

Isabella founded many monasteries and laid the basis of a magnificent royal art collection. Charles V and Philip II both employed Titian, though in other respects Philip's taste was odd (he did not care for El Greco). The Habsburgs perhaps did not like the Spanish taste for highly decorative art. The palace of Charles V in Granada (1540) was the one Spanish building that truly reflected the ideas of Bramante. Philip demanded a severe, un-Spanish style for the Escorial.

Above: The vast Escorial of Philip II, a granite fortress of Spanish Catholicism, which was a palace, monastery, school, mausoleum, and record office.

Foreign artists

The Renaissance, starting in Italy, happened in different countries at different times. In Spain, despite the early arrival of humanism, the Renaissance belongs to the 16th and early 17th centuries. The outstanding painter in Spain was El Greco (the Greek, 1541–1614), who was born in Crete (which belonged to Venice). He came to Spain hoping for court patronage, but his strange, passionate Mannerist style did not appeal to Philip II, and he died unrecognized as the genius he was.

Right: Detail from Titian's Diana and Acteon. Unlike his father, Philip liked paintings from Classical mythology, especially with attractive females.

Below: The European dominions of Charles V. After his abdication, the lands were divided between a Spanish branch (Philip II) and a German branch (the Emperor Ferdinand I, Charles' brother).

Right: Detail from El Greco's painting of St. Martin and the Beggar.

Left: Prince Henry (1394–1460), a brother of the Portuguese king, was called "The Navigator" by the English. He encouraged Portuguese captains seeking a route to the East Indies.

Portugal

That Portugal remained independent under its royal Aviz dynasty while Spain was unified was largely a matter of chance. Castile had more in common with Portugal than some parts of Spain (for instance, Catalonia). But when Philip II inherited the crown of Portugal in 1580, the Portuguese had gained a strong sense of their nationhood, due in part to their creation of a rich commercial empire in the East. They regained their independence in 1640.

Right: The Belém Tower, guarding Lisbon harbor, built in the Portuguese late-Gothic style called Manueline (after King Manuel, reigned 1495–1521).

Boundary of dominions of Charles V

Inheritance of Philip II

NETHERLANDS

FRANCHE-COMTE

PORTUGAL

SPAIN

ARAGON

CASTILE

Granada •

SARDINIA

• Rome

Naples •

MEDITERRANEAN SEA

SICILY

Indulgences

One symptom of the rot that had set in the Church was the growing sale of indulgences. These were bits of paper bearing a promise that people who bought them would have their sins forgiven. To intelligent people, indulgences were a trick to obtain money out of simple people. Luther, a scholarly Saxon monk, attacked them in a paper that he nailed to a church door in Wittenberg on October 31, 1517. His protest marks the start of the Reformation, which split Christian Europe in two.

Left: Buying an indulgence was supposed to reduce the time your soul would spend in purgatory after your death.

Luther preaching. A tireless teacher, he published books and pamphlets for thirty years.

Martin Luther

Luther (1483–1546) believed that sinners won God's forgiveness through the power of God's love, which they could gain only by their personal faith in God. Gifts to charity, Church rituals, priests, and prayers had nothing to do with it. *Sola fide,* which is Latin for "by faith alone," was his message. God's will was to be read in the Bible, not interpreted by pope or priest. Luther's beliefs struck at the whole institution of the Roman Church.

The Reformation

The Church became unpopular in the 15th century. People were no less religious, but many were disgusted with the clergy, from the Pope downward. Most Renaissance popes behaved no better than any other ambitious prince. Bishops were often greedy, living lives of luxury and not bothering to visit their dioceses. Many clergy were dishonest or ignorant. No one wanted to destroy the Church, only reform it, but what started as a protest turned into a revolution. The protesters ("Protestants") found that they disagreed not just with the customs of the Church but with its basic beliefs. State churches were created apart from, and hostile to, the Church of Rome. They were still Christian, but it was a different kind of Christianity.

Defender of the Church

Traditionally, the secular defender of Christendom was the Holy Roman Emperor. As emperor, Charles V (reigned 1519–1556) was also king of Germany, although in practice he had little control of the German princes. Some of the princes saw political advantages in converting to Lutheranism. They gained more power, greater independence, and great wealth from confiscated Church property. Of course, many were also sincere converts.

Johann Eck, a theologian, opened the attack on Luther by accusing him of heresy, which made the quarrel public and led to the showdown at Worms.

The Diet of Worms

Both Pope and Emperor hoped to avoid a major crisis, but in 1521, after Luther had refused to withdraw his views, the Pope excommunicated him. Weeks later he was summoned to the imperial diet, an assembly of representatives of the German states, with the emperor himself presiding. Luther again refused to back down and was declared an outlaw. Any hope of a compromise had gone and the Church was permanently split.

Divisions of doctrine

What made the division in the Church impossible to resolve were disagreements over the sacraments. Transubstantiation was the main stumbling block. The Roman Church held that, in the sacrament of the Eucharist, the bread and wine are miraculously changed into the body and blood of Christ. The reformers did not agree. There were also differences over marriage (forbidden to Catholic priests but not to those in the reformed Churches) and baptism.

Above: Charles V and the Elector of Saxony discuss the Confession of Augsburg (1530), a last attempt to reunite the Church.

Protestant propaganda: A saintly Lutheran minister and a corrupt Roman Catholic priest.

The Schmalkaldic League

Rejection of the Confession of Augsburg meant civil war. At Schmalkalden, German Protestant princes, led by Philip of Hesse and the Elector of Saxony, formed an alliance against the emperor. Charles had so many other problems that he did not confront the League until 1547, when his crack Spanish troops routed its army at Muhlberg (1547). In the long run it made no difference. Protestantism remained firmly established in northern Germany.

Below: Luther began his translation of the Bible into German in the Wartburg, which served as a refuge.

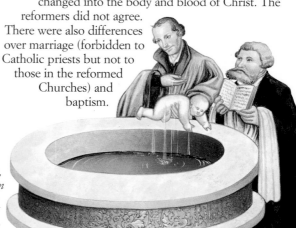

Right: Philipp Melancthon, a layman, baptizes a baby, which in the Roman Church only priests may do. The moderate Melancthon was the chief organizer of Lutheranism and author of the Confession of Augsburg.

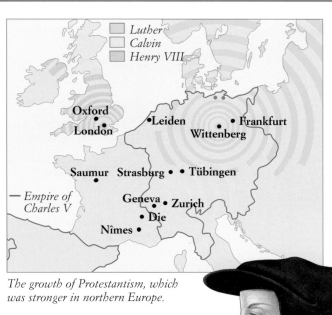

The growth of Protestantism, which was stronger in northern Europe.

Katherina von Bora, a nun, left her convent to become a Lutheran and later married Luther (1525).

Monasteries

Monasteries were in decline in the 15th century. As a result of general discontent with the Church, fewer people became monks and nuns, and in some places they did more partying than praying. But monasteries were rich, and the value of monastic lands was another temptation for rulers to break away from the Church of Rome. Destruction of monasteries angered ordinary people and caused rebellions in England, Sweden, and Germany.

Right: Calvin was a major influence on Protestantism in France, the Netherlands, Scotland, and, later, New England.

Calvin

The French theologian John Calvin (1509–1564) was the most influential reformer after Luther. A generation younger, he rejected Roman Catholicism about 1533. In 1536 he published his famous *Institutes of the Christian Religion*, a clear, comprehensive description of the reformed religion, expressed with great intellectual power and moral passion. His work on Church government, *Ecclesiastical Ordinances* (1541), provided the basis for Presbyterianism.

Zwingli

Ulrich Zwingli (1484–1531), a Swiss priest, was strongly influenced by humanism, especially by Erasmus. He developed beliefs similar to Luther's and converted the people of Zurich to the reformed religion (1523). He was killed when the Catholic cantons attacked Zurich. Leadership of Swiss Protestantism then passed to Calvin.

Above: The ideas of Zwingli had a strong influence on the future Church of England.

Below: Geneva in the 15th century. It became the chief center of Protestantism in the mid-16th century.

A battle of images

All the reformers objected to the Roman Church's use of Latin, its elaborate rituals, rich furnishings, and lavish works of art. The more extreme reformers saw images as interfering with a true relationship with God. The making of images, they said, was condemned in the Bible, because the image itself might become the object of worship. Many beautiful works of art were destroyed by mobs.

Above: Roman Catholic propaganda: the devil's tune comes from Luther-like bagpipes.

Right: Protestant propaganda: The devil's chariot, made out of pope and priests, carries souls off to Hell.

Calvin's Geneva

Calvin created his model church during his 25 years in Geneva. He was a severe moralist, in many ways more strict than the Catholic Church. Like other reformers, he took the Bible as the ultimate authority. He believed that whether a person is damned or saved is decided by God, and the individual has no control over his fate (this doctrine is called predestination). Some later Calvinists, though not Calvin himself, insisted that only the elect (i.e., members of their own church) would be saved.

The Church of England

Henry VIII ended the Pope's authority over the English Church (1534) for political reasons. He needed the pope's approval to divorce his wife and the pope refused it. However, Henry was no Protestant. Although he shut down the monasteries, he wanted to keep the Roman Catholic religion – without Rome. The pope was no longer head of the Church; Henry was. But the reformers had won over many powerful people in England and, after Henry's death (1547), England became a Protestant country.

Left: The title "Defender of the Faith," held by English monarchs, was granted to Henry VIII by the pope in 1521 for writing a book attacking Luther.

Right: Henry VIII dismissed his minister, Cardinal Wolsey (right), when Wolsey failed to persuade the pope to end Henry's marriage.

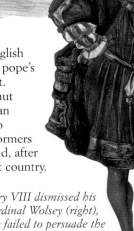

The Low Countries and Germany

Measured by the growth of towns, industry, and trade, the most advanced regions in Europe in the late Middle Ages, after Italy, were the Low Countries and southern Germany. Both regions enjoyed some degree of independence. In Germany, the princely states and Imperial-free cities had no overlord except the remote emperor. The northern cities of the Hanseatic League likewise ran their own affairs. Growing city life and prosperity in the Low Countries and Germany brought advances in technology and a lively culture. Although the Renaissance began in Italy, it depended also on major developments in northern Europe: the first printing press was set up in the Rhineland city of Mainz; the technique of painting in oils was developed in Flanders.

View of a prosperous city in the Low Countries in the 16th century.

Growth of towns

The cities of Flanders, well-placed on a crossroads of trade routes, grew wealthy on the medieval wool trade. The wealth of its merchants and the colorful court of the dukes of Burgundy made Bruges the most dashing city in northern Europe in the 15th century. By 1500 it had been overtaken in importance by Antwerp, and the northern provinces were growing too. Holland was the most urbanized region in Europe; half its people lived in towns.

Left: A drinking horn used at the feasts of a craft guild in the Netherlands.

Above: Wooden figure of St. Nicholas, patron saint of Bruges.

Flemish art

Burgundy's tradition of rich miniature painting (manuscript illustrations), the cultured Burgundian court, and the wealth of the burghers in cities like Bruges, all played a part in the revival of Gothic art in Flanders and the Netherlands in the 15th century. Subjects were mainly religious, with some portraits. Among the greatest artists of the school were Jan van Eyck and Rogier van der Weyden.

Left: Madonna and child by Rogier van der Weyden (1399–1464).

Map of Erasmus' travels

Cambridge
Oxford
Gouda   Deventer
Steyn   NETHERLANDS
London   Antwerp 's-Hertogenbosch
         Louvain   → route
FLANDERS   FRANCE
Cambrai
         Freiburg
Paris   Basel
                    Venice
         Turin
              Bologna
              Florence
              Siena

Merchants

A wealthy merchant of the late Middle Ages would have looked like a prince. In Italy such men sometimes became princes, but in the Low Countries the communal form of government proved stronger. One reason was the weakness of local rulers, who granted special privileges to merchants' and craftsmen's guilds in exchange for their support. Later rulers, trying to impose their authority, ran into a strongly established spirit of independence.

Erasmus hoped to reform the Church by peaceful persuasion, but his hopes were dashed by the Lutheran revolution.

Humanism in the Low Countries

The most powerful influence on humanism in the Low Countries came from a religious society, the Brothers of the Common Life. Many leading figures of the Northern Renaissance were educated at their schools, including Erasmus (1466–1536). Among many learned works, his most popular was *Praise of Folly* (1509), which wittily attacked human superstition and stupidity.

Left: Peasants dancing at a wedding, detail from a painting by Pieter Brueghel the Elder.

Painting everyday life

Italian influence had little effect on Flemish painting until about 1500, when the subject matter of art also widened. The most interesting addition was the painting of everyday life and ordinary people. Pieter Brueghel the Elder (1529–1569), first of a long line of painters, specialized in peasants and country scenes. Hieronymus Bosch (died 1516) painted what we see as weird and sinister scenes, such as malformed people and distorted animals.

Right: The power of the Dutch is suggested by this map (1648) of the United Provinces.

The Dutch republic

The Spanish had other, more powerful enemies, so they signed a truce with the Dutch in 1609 (though they only recognized Dutch independence in 1648). The new Dutch republic, called the United Provinces, was the most democratic state in Europe. The Dutch were seafarers, and in the 17th century they became a formidable commercial power, dominating European trade and winning an empire in Asia, America, and Africa.

A beggar's bowl, symbol of the Dutch rebels, whose leaders had been mocked as beggars by the Spanish.

Revolt of the Netherlands

Calvinism made many converts in the Netherlands. Economic grievances and hatred of the oppressive Catholic government of the Spanish Habsburgs led to general rebellion. The Spanish response was a reign of terror led by the ferocious duke of Alba (1567). In 1579, the southern provinces, where Protestantism was weaker, made peace with Spain, but Holland and the northern provinces fought on.

The Holy Roman Empire

Although the Holy Roman Emperor was elected by leading German princes, in practice he was always a Habsburg. On paper the Empire was the largest state in western Europe, but the German princes ruled independently and resisted attempts to create a centralized state. Under Maximilian I (1459–1519) and Charles V (1519–1556), Habsburg territory was huge, but each part was separate, and the emperor's many duties made him weaker.

Left: Figure of Emperor Maximilian I, who gained Burgundy by marriage, and married his son to the heiress of Spain.

Germany did not have a single currency. Each state minted its own coins.

The peasants' revolt

A huge rebellion broke out in Germany in 1524 due to economic exploitation by landowners, including the Church. It was encouraged by Protestant revolutionaries who preached that the Second Coming of Christ was about to happen. Mobs destroyed castles and churches. Luther condemned the revolt for its mindless violence, and it was finally crushed (1527) by the princes. Thousands of the rebels were

Poor townspeople joined the peasants in their demand for freedom (freiheit).

Boundary of the Holy Roman

Rostock • • Greifswald   PRUSSIA
POLAND
• Frankfurt
Wittenberg •
Louvain • Cologne • • Leipzig
Marburg • Erfurt   SILESIA
Trier • Mainz
Heidelberg • • Würzburg • Prague
FRANCE   BOHEMIA
Tübingen • Dillingen
Freiburg • • Ingolstadt
Besançon • • Vienna
Dôle • Basel
TYROL   HUNGARY

☐ *Habsburg land 1519*   ☐ *area gained in 1526 by Habsburg*

This map shows the major universities in the Holy Roman Empire. Their number more than doubled during the course of the 15th century.

Humanism in Germany

Many learned Germans in the 15th century studied in Italy, where they were influenced by Italian humanism. Their influence in turn, along with that of foreign lecturers (mainly Italian), was passed on through the newly founded German universities, especially Vienna and Heidelberg, and schools like those run by the Brethren of the Common Life. Germany did not have a Classical heritage like Italy, but Germans came to feel pride in their own past.

Portrait by Lucas Cranach of Philipp Melancthon (see page 28), Luther's chief disciple, who was a friend of Erasmus and author of a Greek textbook.

Craftsmanship

The German cities had long been famous for the high standards of their craftsmen in the artistic crafts, gold and silversmiths in particular. Augsburg was especially prosperous in the early 16th century, due partly to its rich banking houses. Nuremberg had an extraordinary number of artist-craftsmen. Among them was the family of Vischer, metalworkers and sculptors, whose works between 1480 and 1520 show the gradual change from Gothic to Renaissance style.

Left: A German drinking vessel made from a nautilus shell set in silver gilt.

Art in Germany

In Germany, the Gothic style was not easily displaced by new ideas from Italy. It is interesting to see how, from about 1470, ideas learned in Italy appeared in decorative details, command of perspective, and so on, but the work as a whole still belonged in spirit to the north. This was a great period for German culture. Germany had no Florence of course, but cities like Ulm and Nuremberg contained both great artists and rich middle-class patrons to employ them.

Right: Detail of an altarpiece by the great painter Mathias Grünewald (1474–1528), a religious mystic who was hostile to Renaissance classicism.

Woodcarving

A strong tradition of realistic sculpture in wood, usually for churches, existed in Bavaria and other forested parts of Germany, mainly the south. Some of the finest artworks of 15th century Germany, such as the altarpieces of Michael Pacher, among others, were painted wooden reliefs. Sculptors such as the strikingly expressive Veit Stoss and the calmer, more restrained Tilmann Riemenschneider worked in wood.

Left: Painted limewood figure of the Virgin and Child by the Würzburg sculptor Tilman Riemenschneider (1460–1531).

Left: Dürer painted a famous series of portraits of himself, here as a young man (1498).

Dürer

Albrecht Dürer (1471–1528) was the greatest German artist of his time and one of the best in Europe. Son of a Nuremberg goldsmith, he visited Venice and was strongly influenced by the great Italians, though his paintings remained recognizably northern in spirit. He was a master of wood engraving, which he raised to a new level of technical excellence. In Italy, the high social status of Italian artists impressed Dürer. Later, he befriended Erasmus and Melancthon.

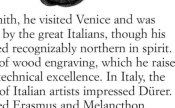

Renaissance France

Right: The kneeling figure in this masterpiece of the goldsmith's art is Charles the Bold, last of the great dukes of Burgundy.

In the early 15th century, the kingdom of France was small. It looked as though it might disappear altogether under the combined attack of England and Burgundy. But, the English were driven out of all their French possessions (except Calais) by 1453, and the death of Charles the Bold, duke of Burgundy, without an heir in 1477 ended the threat from the most powerful of the French lords. France recovered fast from the Hundred Years' War with England, due to the wise policies of Louis XI (1461–1483). Between 1481 and 1492, it more than doubled in size. An agreement made after Charles the Bold's death gave Burgundy to the French king. The death of another great lord added Anjou and Provence. A third fortunate death left the large and independent duchy of Brittany to Anne of Brittany. She had many suitors, among them Louis' successor, Charles VIII. With Charles' army menacing the duchy, Anne could not refuse. But Charles' ambitions went farther. In 1494 he invaded Italy, starting the long conflict with the Habsburgs.

François I strengthened the monarchy by frequent visits to all parts of his kingdom.

François I

François I (reigned 1515–1547) was a true Renaissance prince, though he was also something of a medieval warrior-king. Intelligent, athletic (he once beat Henry VIII of England at wrestling), unscrupulous, and a generous patron of art and learning, he presided over an extravagant court, but wasted large sums on useless wars against Emperor Charles V. He imported Italian artists in droves to work on his architectural projects, including Leonardo da Vinci.

The elegant Gallery of François I (1531) at Fontainebleau, containing some of the finest decoration.

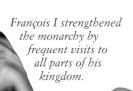

The kingdom

In France, as in England and Spain, the creation of a powerful nation was achieved through a strong monarchy. The nobles, who had challenged – and sometimes overthrown – royal power during the Middle Ages, were finally brought under control. But kings' ambition did not stop at their own boundaries. In 1494, France invaded Italy.

Left: Miniature enamel portrait of the constable of France, Anne de Montmorency, by Léonard Limousin (died 1576), an outstanding artist in this type of work.

This map shows the expansion of the French kingdom between the end of the Hundred Years' War (1453) and the Treaty of Cateau-Cambrésis (1559), which ended the Italian wars.

France, 1453	
area annexed	
Habsburg dominions, 1559	
French boundary, 1559	—

Châteaux of the Loire

The valley of the River Loire is famous for its châteaux (castles). Many of their splendors are due to François I. Perhaps the finest is Chambord, with its staggering array of towers and spires which, unlike most others, was built from scratch, rather than altered, and was designed by an Italian. Even more famous is Fontainebleau, originally a medieval hunting lodge, which François made into a huge, rambling palace the size of a small town.

The School of Fontainebleau

The influential French Renaissance school takes its name from the decoration of the palace by Italian artists, including Rosso – who designed the Gallery of François I – and Primaticcio. Much of it is a masterly and new combination of woodwork, molded stucco (including huge curling scrolls), and painting, mainly illustrating Classical subjects. The human figures are sinuous and elegant. This extravagant style is usually described as Mannerist (a cross between Renaissance and Baroque).

Left: Painting in enamel of the god Apollo, at Fontainebleau.

Italian influence: Detail of a painting by Antoine Caron, who had worked at Fontainebleau under Primaticcio. It shows the Colosseum in Rome.

The new Louvre

The Louvre in Paris was originally a fort, which grew over the centuries and was turned into a splendid palace in the 16th century. François I, who began it, knew the importance of having a royal presence in the capital and made it the seat of his court (though the court usually preferred to stay elsewhere). The artists responsible were the learned Pierre Lescot, whose buildings around a square courtyard show a thorough understanding of the Italian models he had in mind and influenced the development of French classicism, and the sculptor Jean Goujon, also Italian-influenced.

Above: The Hall of the Caryatids was based on a Greek temple, the Erectheion, in Athens.

Humanism in France

Scholarship in France was conservative, but there was a humanist circle at the Sorbonne around Robert Gaguin, who set up a printing press (1470) and attracted foreign scholars, mainly Italians. The leading thinker, Lefèvre d'Étaples, was a humanist theologian; Guillaume Budé was a renowned classical scholar. One undoubted humanist was that extravagant literary genius, François Rabelais (died 1553), whose humor was directed at every human activity, especially the Church.

Building of the Louvre and nearby Tuileries continued into the reign of Henri IV.

Jean Clouet's portrait of Guillaume Budé (1468–1540). Budé got François I to found the Collège de France (1530) as a modern center of learning.

Below: Terracotta medallions like this, in the style of Renaissance Florence, decorated many French buildings.

Henri II and Catherine de Médicis

The last Valois kings of France reigned in troubled times that included the savage French Religious Wars (see page 34), for which they were partly responsible. Henri II (reigned 1547–1559) succeeded his father, François I. He married the lively Catherine, a princess of the Medici dynasty and another keen patron of the arts (she designed the chateaux herself). His court was split by fierce rivalry between two aristocratic families, Montmorency and Guise, and his sale of government posts bankrupted the monarchy. His three sons (1559–1589) were weak rulers. They were dominated by their mother, Catherine, whose policy was guided by her determination to preserve the throne for her sons at all costs.

Below: The beautiful Fontaine des Innocents was designed by Jean Goujon to celebrate the entry of Henri II into Paris.

Italian influence

The Italian influence on the Renaissance in France began in the 15th century and accelerated after the French invasion, when Frenchmen saw Italian cities first hand. It grew stronger under François I. The school of Fontainebleau was predominantly Italian: Primaticcio was recommended to François by the duke of Mantua. Overall, however, the results were distinctively French, and thereafter the influence of Italy, where the High Renaissance was long past, was less obvious. The portraits of Jean Clouet suggest a Flemish heritage, and after 1550 it is more difficult to distinguish strictly Italian influences. There was a definite reaction against the Italians in the time of Catherine de Médicis, whose many Italian relations and hangers-on were not popular at the French court.

Below: The Pont Neuf, Paris's first classical bridge (1578–1589).

Above: Portrait of Charles IX (reigned 1560–1574), second son of Henri II, by François Clouet, who followed his father, Jean, as court painter in 1541.

Right: Classical figure in bronze, commissioned to decorate the Pont Neuf.

Renaissance Paris

Medieval Paris, like other medieval cities, was a jumble of narrow streets and tall, timber-framed, gabled buildings, with no special effort to match one building with its neighbors. They were the work of builders. With the Renaissance, the architects took over. New developments were not just built, they were designed. An important feature was the new idea of perspective, which encouraged the building of squares, lined with uniform buildings (often with arcades), a statue or fountain in the center, and streets radiating off. Of course, the new ideas only affected small bits of a large city such as Paris. Examples built under Henri IV were the Place Royal (Place des Vosges) and the Place Dauphine.

Counter Reformation and Religious Wars

The saintly Teresa of Avila (1515–1582) founded the reformed branch (both monks and nuns) of the Carmelite order.

Charles Borromeo (1538–1584) was a leader of Roman Catholic reform and a powerful supporter of the work of the Council of Trent.

The Reformation split the Church yet, in a way, it made Rome stronger than before. Threatened with destruction by the Reformers, the Roman Church fought back. Reforms that nearly everyone agreed were necessary were at last carried out. In the war of religious propaganda, Rome found defenders like Johann Eck, who were as persuasive as Luther. Many people found consolation in the certainties of the old religion. which Lutheranism did not provide. There were two sides of the Counter-Reformation. The negative side, represented by the Inquisition and the Index, attacked all forms of heresy, including quite mild criticism that would not have bothered the old Church. The positive side included the reform of religious doctrine in the work of the Council of Trent, the ending of abuses such as indulgences (which had provoked Luther's first attack), and the establishment of higher standards among the clergy.

New orders

Religious orders revived and new ones were founded that were more active in society: the Capuchins worked among the poor, the Ursuline nuns strove for girls' education. Most important was the Society of Jesus (Jesuits), founded by an extraordinary man, Ignatius Loyola, whose *Spiritual Exercises* became the basis of Jesuit training. Approved by Paul III in 1540, the order concentrated on teaching and missionary work. The Jesuits were the cutting edge of the anti-Protestant campaign and regained many converts for Rome.

Loyola with Pope Paul III, who approved the Jesuit order, though many (including Paul IV) distrusted it.

The new papacy

A major target for the attacks of Reformers was the character of the Renaissance popes, most of them greedy, worldly and ungodly. Plenty of good men existed, even among bishops, but strong leadership from the top was essential. Pope Paul III (1534–1549) had many of his predecessors' vices, but he recognized the need for reform and appointed able reformers to high office. Chief of them was the fierce Cardinal Carafa, later Paul IV (1555–1559), who was responsible, among other reforms, for the Index (1543), which banned all books of which the Church disapproved.

Below: The Council of Trent, which met in three sessions between 1545 and 1563, created the basis of the Counter Reformation.

Right: A vision of the Roman Church as a fortress, defending the faith against Protestant heresy.

Council of Trent

Popes usually feared general councils of the Church because they threatened papal authority, but the overhaul of doctrine – the beliefs and teaching of the Church – was too much for the pope to handle alone. So the Council of Trent was formed. The output of the Council was enormous. It mainly concerned doctrine, condemning Luther's justification by faith, and making firm decisions on all points of disagreement. The result was to make belief clearer and the Church more unified. Strongly anti-Protestant, it confirmed the permanent division in Christianity and the start of a new, narrower, modern Roman Catholic Church as one of several Christian sects.

Catholic mobs slaughtered thousands of Huguenots in the St. Bartholomew's Day Massacre.

The Inquisition

The Roman Inquisition was reformed in 1542 at the urging of Cardinal Carafa, who became its head. It was modeled on the successful Spanish Inquisition. Its powers against heresy were sweeping and included supervision of the religious orders, bringing them under closer papal control. When Carafa became pope (at age 80) he turned up the pressure, even prosecuting good Catholics who dared suggest that the Church and papacy were not perfect. He rooted out all heresy in Italy, but the price was the ruin of Italian intellectual life and the end of the Italian Renaissance.

Victim of the Spanish Inquisition (see page 26) wearing the tunic of the condemned.

The religious settlement in England

In England, Henry VIII had created a state church but kept the traditional doctrine. Under Edward VI (1547–1553), the English Church became Protestant, but Edward died young and was succeeded by his sister Mary I (1553–1558), a devoted Catholic. She restored the old religion and papal control – and married the Catholic champion, Philip II of Spain. A few Protestants, including three bishops, were burned as heretics. It was left to Elizabeth I (1558–1603) to make a final settlement of the Church of England as independent and Protestant – but with bishops, and in doctrine closer to Rome than other Protestant Churches.

French religious wars

Between 1562 and 1598, France was torn by a series of civil conflicts. The root cause was an aristocratic power struggle for control of the failing Valois dynasty. The chief opponents were Catholic extremists and leaders of the Huguenots (Protestants, a large minority). Various foreign powers intervened at times on both sides. In 1572 a plot to kill the Huguenot leaders, approved by Catherine de Médicis got out of hand and resulted in the Massacre of St. Bartholomew's Day. Afterwards, a moderate Catholic party led by the Montmorencys, strived for tolerance. But the extremists – led by the Guises – formed the Holy League, which grew more relentless when Henri of Navarre, the Huguenot leader, became heir to the throne.

ENGLAND
☐ *area in which Protestantism was accepted*

HOLY ROMAN EMPIRE

— *boundaries of France*

● Rouen
Paris ● ● Meaux
Orléans ● Troyes ●
Angers ● SWISS CONFEDERATION
Saumur ● ● la Charité
Bourges ●

● Lyon

FRANCE

areas of Huguenot concentration
☐ high ● Bordeaux
☐ medium Albi ●
☐ low Toulouse ● ● Gaillac

SPAIN

This map shows the locations of the St. Bartholomew's Day massacres.

Right: Under the Thirty-nine Articles (1563), which established the belief and practices of the Church of England, the monarch was named as supreme governor.

Below: Henri IV, first of the Bourbon dynasty, married a Valois princess in 1572, hoping (in vain) to end the religious conflict.

Left: Thousands died in Alba's Council of Blood; in some towns most of the population was executed.

Above: A copy of the Edict of Nantes, which granted some religious toleration to the Huguenots.

Henri IV

The last of the French Religious Wars is called the War of the Three Henrys (King Henri III, Duke Henri of Guise, and Henri of Navarre). It ended in 1589, when the first two were assassinated and Henri of Navarre became king. Although the Huguenots controlled most of France, Catholic Paris still stood out against Henri IV, so he converted to Catholicism, but issued the Edict of Nantes (1598), ending the religious wars. Just, sensible, and popular, he was the first strong king to reign in France for fifty years. His reign (1589–1610) prepared the way for France's rise to predominance in Europe under his grandson, Louis XIV.

The Dutch Protestants

In the Spanish-ruled Netherlands, the Reformation was successful. Calvinism claimed many converts, in spite of persecution by the local Inquisition. Philip II of Spain regarded himself as the defender of Roman Catholicism, and when the Dutch nobles, Catholic and Protestant, demanded religious toleration, Philip refused. Religious opposition then became joined with hatred of Spanish rule. Economic distress and the Calvinist ministers' preaching set off a popular rebellion in 1566. Mob violence disgusted moderates and the rebellion was crushed, but the savagery of the campaign of punishment waged by the duke of Alba in 1567–1573 (see page 30) ended all chance of agreement.

Art and the Counter-Reformation

By about 1550, the classicism of Italian Renaissance art had been abandoned for Mannerism. Human figures were distorted, composition deliberately unbalanced, and vivid colors heightened the emotional effect. After 1600 it gave way to Baroque, exploiting every trick of illusionism and becoming even more intensely emotional. These developments suited the new, aggressive Roman Catholic Church, which saw the purpose of art as religious propaganda and demanded intense feeling and spectacular effects.

The Renaissance Man

When someone is described today as a Renaissance Man (or woman), it means he is skilled in more than one subject. Human knowledge has increased so much that a modern expert is nearly always a specialist in a small field. In the Renaissance, artists were interested in all the arts, including the decorative arts and what we should call crafts, which were not yet generally seen as inferior to the fine arts. Often they were interested in non-artistic subjects too. Leonardo has been call the first scientist. Michelangelo signed himself Michelangelo, sculptor, but his best-known work is a painting, and he was also a fine poet as well as the architect of St. Peter's, Rome. They are the two giants of the Renaissance (though they did not like each other much and were once embarrassed to find themselves working in the same room).

Above: Detail from Verrocchio's Baptism of Christ, *Leonardo's angel on the left.*

Above: Leonardo's famous drawing to show the proportions of the human body, based on Vitruvius.

The young Leonardo
Leonardo da Vinci (1452–1519) was born in a village near Florence. His father was a prominent lawyer who, upon seeing his talent, had him apprenticed to the leading Florentine artist, Andrea del Verrocchio. He remained in Verrocchio's studio for twelve years, long after he became fully qualified. A legend says that Verrocchio (primarily a sculptor) was so impressed by an angel painted by Leonardo for one of Verrocchio's pictures, he swore to give up painting.

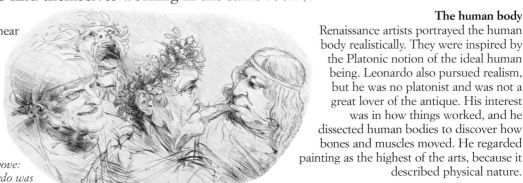

Above: Leonardo was fascinated by faces, especially craggy, even grotesque types.

The human body
Renaissance artists portrayed the human body realistically. They were inspired by the Platonic notion of the ideal human being. Leonardo also pursued realism, but he was no platonist and was not a great lover of the antique. His interest was in how things worked, and he dissected human bodies to discover how bones and muscles moved. He regarded painting as the highest of the arts, because it described physical nature.

A page from his notebooks. Because he was left-handed, Leonardo wrote backwards, from right to left, so that a mirror is needed to read it.

Paintings (portraiture)
Only about ten paintings by Leonardo survive. A perfectionist, he often left projects and paintings unfinished, partly because he was less interested in the finished painting as a work of art than in how it was achieved. His spirit of invention led him to experiment with techniques. And, unfortunately, they often failed. His greatest painting, *The Last Supper*, was one casualty. It soon deteriorated, and has been often restored – by hands less skilful than his.

Above: Leonardo invented a new kind of portrait. This is his most famous, the Mona Lisa, *with her mysterious smile – a Leonardo trademark.*

Left: A modern model of a centrally planned church, based on Leonardo's drawing for Pavia Cathedral.

Writings
Leonardo filled thousands of pages of notes on every field of science, accompanied by sketches. Many of his writings have survived, though no one, and certainly not Leonardo himself, ever managed to organize them. The rediscovery of his writings in the last century explains his reputation today as not just a great artist but a pioneer of science and the greatest creative mind of his time. To Leonardo, art and science were not separate, they were both part of the search for knowledge.

Leonardo's portrait of an old man, which scholars believe is probably a self-portrait.

The engineer
Leonardo studied hundreds of technological problems, from grinding lenses to diverting the course of a river. He was especially fascinated by the power of water and the possibility of flight. He gained the patronage of the duke of Milan by his ability as a musician and military engineer and by promising that he could make a huge statue in bronze of a warrior on horseback. It would have been the biggest in the world, but he only got as far as the model.

A model made from Leonardo's sketch of a kind of tank, driven by horses inside. Like his flying machines, it was never built.

Artists followed their patrons. Leonardo's most productive years were in Milan; Michelangelo's in Rome.

- Amboise
- Venice
- Milan
- Mantua
- Parma
- Florence
- Rome

Leonardo's Timeline
1452 Born near Vinci	the *Adoration of the Magi*, earliest large surviving work	casting bronze horse	Isabella d'Este in Mantua	*Rocks*
1470 In Verrocchio's workshop, Florence	1482 Enters the service of Duke Ludovico of Milan	1495 Begins *The Last Supper*	1502 Appointed architect and engineer to Cesare Borgia	1513 Based in Rome
1480 Preparatory cartoon of	1491 Describes method for	1499 Leaves Milan after French occupation	1503 Starts *Mona Lisa*	1517 Invited to settle in France by François I
		1500 Makes drawing of	1507 Completes *Virgin of the*	1519 Dies in France

Michelangelo

The monumental yet very personal art of Michelangelo was inspired by the two main influences on his character. First was the platonist humanism of the Medici court, where he grew up after Lorenzo de Medici noticed his talent in the sculpture school. Second was his deep but troubled faith in a pure and simple Christianity, as taught by Savonarola. These very different views of life caused him mental pain, but in his art they produced the intense emotion that fired his genius.

Like others, Michelangelo studied remains of antique sculpture in search of Classical perfection. He saw the human body as God's finest expression.

Rome

Before the French invasion, Michelangelo left Florence and spent five years in Rome. When he returned he was famous. His *Pièta* (see page 21) was hailed by all as a work of genius. Back in Florence, his colossal marble David (see page 7) confirmed his fame. Courts all over Italy begged him to work for them. He took on more than he could do, especially large-scale projects, and many would-be patrons were disappointed (the duke of Mantua pursued him in vain for eleven years).

Figure of Moses from the tomb of Julius II.

Paintings

Michelangelo's few paintings are rather like sculpture in two dimensions. He said that painting and sculpture are basically the same thing and the object of both is to make figures. His subject was always the human body, particularly the male nude. He was not interested in rich drapery or picturesque ruins, and despised Flemish painting. His idea of good painting was to copy the perfections of God, who made Man in his own image.

Right: Detail of Michelangelo's earliest known painting (1503–1504), a circular panel of the Holy Family.

The tomb of Julius II

In 1505 Michelangelo was summoned to Rome to make a tomb for Pope Julius II. He planned a magnificent set-piece in marble with about fifty life-size human figures. The job lasted, off and on, for forty years – long after Julius was dead. First, the pope changed his mind, then the money ran out, and then the right marble was not available. The design changed at least five times, each version smaller than the last. Bored, tired, and angry, Michelangelo regarded the final result as a bitter failure.

Bronze bust of Michelangelo by Daniele da Volterra, one of many artists who aspired to portray the great master.

Below: The dome of St. Peter's was designed by Michelangelo, though built after his death in a slightly different form.

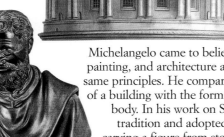

The Sistine Chapel

In 1508 Julius II persuaded Michelangelo to paint the vault (ceiling) of the pope's chapel in the Vatican, the Sistine Chapel. The subject, chosen by the artist, is the origins of humanity as told in the Bible, and the theme is Christian salvation. The work took four years, and Michelangelo wrote amusingly about the physical difficulties: bending backwards on a platform 65 feet (20 m) up, paint dripping in his face, unable to get far enough away from the surface to see what he was doing.

Figures representing Night *and* Day *from the tomb of Giuliano de' Medici, part of Michelangelo's (unfinished) Medici funeral chapel in St. Lorenzo, Florence.*

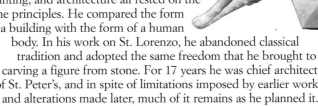

Architecture

Michelangelo came to believe that sculpture, painting, and architecture all rested on the same principles. He compared the form of a building with the form of a human body. In his work on St. Lorenzo, he abandoned classical tradition and adopted the same freedom that he brought to carving a figure from stone. For 17 years he was chief architect of St. Peter's, and in spite of limitations imposed by earlier work and alterations made later, much of it remains as he planned it.

Michelangelo's Timeline			
1475 Born near Florence	household	1508 Begins Sistine Chapel vault	(Sistine Chapel)	1553 Vasari's biography of Michelangelo published
1488 Enters Medici sculpture school	1496 First visit to Rome	1520 Begins Medici Chapel and library, St. Lorenzo	1545 Ends work on Julius II's tomb	1562 Begins *Rondanini Pièta* (last work)
1490 Joins the Medici	1499 Completes *Pièta* (St. Peter's)	1536 Begins *Last Judgment*	1547 Appointed architect of St. Peter's	1564 Dies in Rome
	1501 Begins *David* (Florence)			

The Renaissance Artist

According to legend, St. Luke, author of the Christian Gospel and patron saint of artists, painted an icon of the Virgin Mary.

The Renaissance is unique in European history for producing such a vast and sustained period of brilliance in the visual arts. Capable, even outstanding artists in 15th century Florence seem to have been as common as shopkeepers. There is no simple explanation for this extraordinary outburst of talent. The circumstances of the time—peace, prosperity, humanist thinking, plenty of rich patrons, intense interest in the ancients, and a new belief in progress—all helped to stimulate the cultural blossoming of the Renaissance. Renaissance art makes a strong impact on us, but we should not separate it from other developments. The same spirit of inquiry that lay behind the art of the Renaissance was responsible for the upheaval of the Reformation and the ocean voyages of the discoverers. These were exciting times.

Right: Terracotta plaque by Della Robbia of the sign of the artists' guild in Florence.

Left: Among the 60 figures that appear on his stone tabernacle in St. Lorenz, Nuremberg (1496), the sculptor Adam Krafft portrayed himself as a devout worker.

The status of the artist
The names of great medieval artists are often unknown, but in the Renaissance, artists took to signing their works. The successful artist was no longer a simple craft worker employed by a local patron. He was an important, often rich, and independent person. As a free agent, usually heading a team of assistants, he was courted by popes and princes. Michelangelo, not the pope, decided the subject of the Sistine Chapel vault, and when the pope came to ask how the work was going, he sometimes got a sharp answer.

Giorgio Vasari (1511–1574), self-portrait. He regarded Michelangelo as the greatest artist.

Self-portraits
In their paintings of religious or mythological scenes, Renaissance artists often included their patrons and themselves among the crowd portraits of living people. As portraits were so popular, artists also portrayed themselves individually. Alberti made a bronze plaque of himself (see page 16). Ghiberti's head appears on his bronze doors for Florence Baptistery. Dürer painted his own portrait many times (see page 31).

Right: Self-portrait of the Venetian Mannerist painter Palma Giovane.

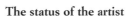

Lives of the artists
The high status of artists was shown by Vasari's *Lives of the Artists* (1550). Vasari was a painter and architect, but his writings are his most valuable legacy. His book was a history of Italian Renaissance art in the form of biographies of leading artists, which were modeled on ancient Greek and Roman lives of famous men. It was the first book in European history entirely about art and artists, and its basic message was that art is an intellectual activity practiced by individuals of genius.

The workshop
A successful artist ran a large studio with assistants and apprentices, who often worked as a team. A big workshop like Verrocchio's in Florence produced many kinds of objects. Verrocchio, like many Renaissance artists, was a qualified goldsmith, as well as a sculptor and painter. Among the variety of objects his workshop provided was the golden ball on the summit of Florence Cathedral. Leonardo probably learned music there, and began his lifelong studies of mathematics and engineering.

A young artist works on a sketch while an apprentice grinds pigments to a fine powder.

Panel painting
Most Old Master paintings are done in oil on canvas, but these materials reached Italy quite late. Although artists like Perugino adopted oil paint exclusively in the 15th century, it was not common in Italy until the mid-16th century. Similarly, easel paintings and altarpieces were often on wooden panels, rather than stretched canvas. Large panels were usually made by a professional carpenter from boards pegged together, and there were many stages between bare wood and final varnish.

Right: Main steps in a panel painting, from top right: treated wood, gesso base (plaster mixed with glue), underdrawing, gold leaf, underpainting, final painting.

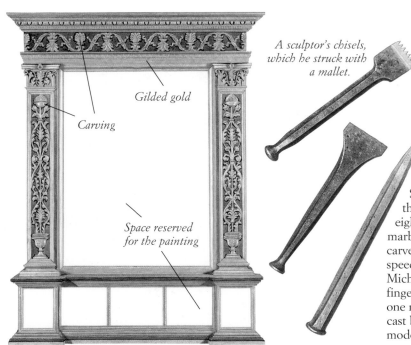

Gilded gold

Carving

Space reserved for the painting

Classical frame for a Renaissance painting.

A sculptor's chisels, which he struck with a mallet.

Sculpture by Michelangelo, showing how the figure emerges from the stone. In its unfinished state, it suggests a human soul struggling to escape from the body.

Sculpture

The aim of Renaissance artists was to portray the reality of the human body, and it could be said that sculpture was the best means (Michelangelo thought it was). Sculptors worked in stone or bronze. They selected their blocks of stone with care: Michelangelo spent eight months in the Carrara quarries choosing marble for Julius II's tomb. His gigantic David was carved from a single block, and he worked at great speed. It has been said that with one blow Michelangelo brought down fragments three or four fingers wide exactly at the point marked, although one mistake could ruin the work. Early bronzes were cast by a professional bronze-caster from a wax model, but sculptors soon set up their own foundries.

Frames

The frame of a picture, elaborately carved and gilded, was almost as important as the painting itself. Some frames for altarpieces cost nearly as much as the painting. In some cases the frame was already present when the painting was done (as in the picture of St. Luke, above) and, especially in the Low Countries, frame and panel were part of the same piece of wood, with or without added molding in stucco.

Lapis lazuli, a stone, provided a deep blue color, often used for the Virgin Mary's cloak. It cost more than gold.

Frescoes

A fresco, from the Italian "fresh," is a type of wall-painting by the ancient Romans as well as Renaissance painters. The paint was watercolor. Although it was possible to work on dry plaster in tempera (pigments bound with egg yolk), painting on wet plaster lasted much longer. Because of a chemical reaction as the plaster dried, the colors became part of the actual wall. Since plaster dried quickly, only a small patch could be done at a time. The technique depended on climate; Florence was ideal, but Venice less so.

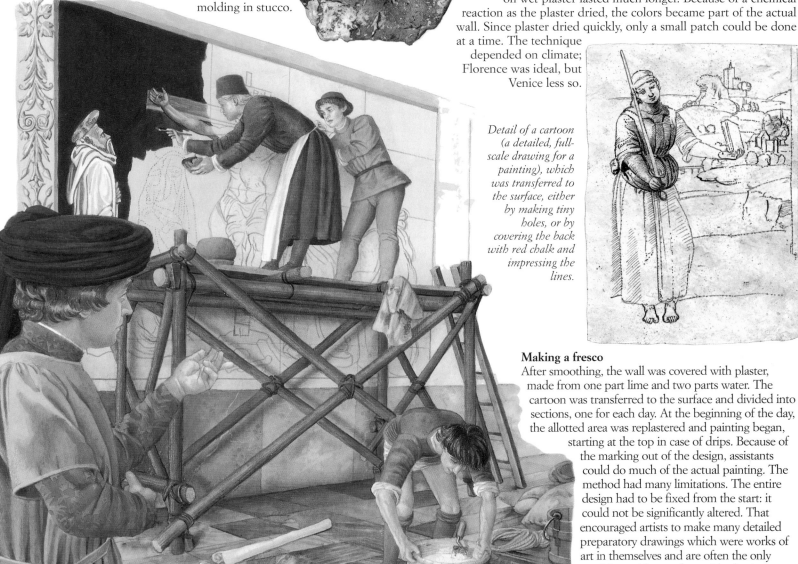

Detail of a cartoon (a detailed, full-scale drawing for a painting), which was transferred to the surface, either by making tiny holes, or by covering the back with red chalk and impressing the lines.

Making a fresco

After smoothing, the wall was covered with plaster, made from one part lime and two parts water. The cartoon was transferred to the surface and divided into sections, one for each day. At the beginning of the day, the allotted area was replastered and painting began, starting at the top in case of drips. Because of the marking out of the design, assistants could do much of the actual painting. The method had many limitations. The entire design had to be fixed from the start: it could not be significantly altered. That encouraged artists to make many detailed preparatory drawings which were works of art in themselves and are often the only surviving evidence of a vanished painting. Colors were limited, and shadows or dark tones were difficult (hence the bright colors of Florentine 15th century frescoes).

Country villa of the Medici in Tuscany.

Wealthy houses

A man's home was a status symbol, a sign of his wealth and importance. Luxury and extravagance were displayed on a grand scale in the princely courts of Italy, but not only princes were rich. On a more modest scale, the houses of German bankers or Flemish merchants demonstrated the new wealth of their owners (and kept the best artists and craftsmen employed). Hampton Court, the grandest house in England, was built (1515–1525) for Cardinal Wolsey, a butcher's son. Houses in general were more comfortable, had better heating (thanks to stoves), more elaborate furniture, and glass windows.

The hearth of a 15th century French house. Wood-burning fires were the chief means of heating and cooking.

Life and Culture in the Renaissance

In 1552 the French writer Rabelais compared the Renaissance with the coming of spring after the long winter of the Middle Ages. While the life of peasants in the fields did not greatly change (though they had more freedom), life for educated people opened up with the recovery of ancient civilization, marking the start of a major change in European culture. Humanism encouraged the inventive advances that were made in every branch of knowledge, from law and mathematics to politics and war and, of course, in art. What people most admired in Renaissance art was its realism: people looked as though they were alive. Humanism taught that people should be guided by honor and tolerance, not just religious obedience. The chivalrous medieval knight was giving way to the gentleman-courtier, who was a man of wide interests, a scholar, and connoisseur.

Fountain with figures of river gods in the gardens of the Villa Farnese, near Rome.

Gardens

The Italian formal style of garden developed in the 16th century, partly based on descriptions of gardens in ancient Rome. The garden was a a work of art that demonstrated human control of nature, and was to be looked at more than strolled in. Flowers and plants were less admired for themselves, and the garden was as much architectural as natural. It was planned on an axis with geometric flower beds and features such as terraces, colonnades, balustrades. It sometimes included sculptures, water pools, and elaborate fountains, like the famous ones in the Villa d'Este at Tivoli or the Villa Farnese.

The courtier

Vergero's *On the Conduct of Honorable Men* (1402) was one of the first of many books that described the ideal qualities of a gentleman. The most popular—a European bestseller—was *The Courtier* by Baldassare Castiglione (1478–1529). It was based on conversations at the highly civilized court of Duke Federico of Urbino from 1504–1508. It presented a picture of the ideal gentleman: courageous, loyal, learned, witty, and pious (much like Castiglione himself, whom Emperor Charles V called "one of the finest gentlemen in the world").

Portrait (about 1540) of a young gentleman, who seems to have interrupted his reading to pose for the painter, Bronzino.

Below: A chair from a wealthy household. Before the 15th century, most people sat on stools.

A painting (1528) by Holbein of his wife and children.

Rising living standards

In a society where the people at the top grow richer, it can happen that some of the wealth percolates downward to benefit people lower down the social scale. According to one writer, ordinary farmers and skilled workers now had silver plates instead of pewter and slept in four-poster beds instead of straw mattresses on the floor! A rise in demand for food helped the farmers, and the creation of new jobs in the towns helped skilled workers. It also opened more jobs to women, though usually at a humble level. Greater opportunities gave people more control over their own lives.

Families

On farms and in urban craft shops, the household was also the center of production, which helped to strengthen family life. There was little privacy: most people shared beds. But, because people generally died younger than now and only one child in four lived to grow up, family life was often broken up. A different attitude to children began to develop. They were understood better as children, instead of undeveloped adults. Boys were still favored, especially in education.

Left: A toiletry box made of precious materials, which belonged to a Venetian lady about 1550.

Leisure

Growing wealth increased people's leisure time. Hunting was still the favorite sport of the ruling class: some of François I's finest castles were hunting lodges, built close to deer forests. Ordinary people were barred. They were not even allowed to kill the wild animals that ate their crops. Jousting, dueling, and archery were still popular, and not only with the nobility. People also enjoyed less violent pastimes, such as chess, cards, and reading. Villagers played a primitive kind of football. Numerous religious festivals provided holidays (Holy days), and regular fairs and carnivals offered a good day out.

Falconry, hunting birds with tame hawks, was a popular sport.

Above: A traveling games box, containing boards for chess, backgammon, and other games.

Courtiers dancing at the wedding feast of a daughter of the Emperor Charles V (1536).

Music

Changes in music during the Renaissance were almost as dramatic as changes in painting and sculpture. Most music in the Middle Ages was religious, but in the 15th–16th centuries it became the most widely popular of all cultural pleasures. Ships on long voyages carried musicians, and every craft or occupation had its own songs. Music was part of the educational curriculum, printed music could be bought, and all educated people could play an instrument (Lorenzo de' Medici recommended Leonardo to the Duke of Milan not as a painter or inventor but as a musician).

Entertainment

Princely courts in the Renaissance put on the most extravagant entertainments since Roman times. They were, of course, demonstrations of the power and wealth of the hosts, who called on the talents of artists and craftsmen to create ingenious devices (Leonardo devoted much time to court festivities in Milan). Besides feasting, they included singing, dancing, and early forms of theater, with sideshows featuring jugglers, acrobats, and others. The origins of opera and ballet can be traced back to these courtly entertainments, where the food, though lavish, was often a minor item. Almost any excuse was enough for a feast, and they sometimes lasted for days.

Waiters in livery at a Medici feast, from a painting by Botticelli (died 1510).

Ladies entertain a court with a lute (like a guitar) and pan-pipes (ancestor of the flute). Violins appeared after 1550.

The shape of this 14th-century French music sheet reflects its subject, a love song.

War

"Must everything be battles...?" asked a Spanish poet in 1589. Almost everyone agreed, reluctantly or not, that war was a condition of life. It was unavoidable. Rulers were held to blame, and rightly so. The earliest kings were tribal warlords, and war continued to be the king's business into modern times. Kings were egged on by their nobles, the descendants of the old warlords, and lieutenants. War did have its advantages. For kings and nobles it brought, if successful, land and thus prestige. Soldiers could profit from looting. However, it also had drawbacks. In 1548 Emperor Charles V wrote a lengthy note of guidance for his son and successor, Philip II, stating that war exhausts the treasury and causes great misery. He went on to list likely causes of conflict that Philip would have to deal with. They included nearly every country in Europe—except Scotland, which was too small and too far away to cause trouble.

An Italian condottiere, *or general.*

Drawing by Leonardo of a ballista, *a giant crossbow used in ancient times. Cannons would soon make such weapons obsolete.*

Weapons

The most important new weapon of the late Middle Ages was the crossbow, which fired a bolt that could penetrate armor at close range. It was rather like a mechanical gun. The bowman pulled a trigger to release a powerful spring that fired the bolt. The English longbow was in some ways a better weapon, but it required great expertise. The inventive spirit of the Renaissance encouraged military engineers, especially useful advising on siege warfare. Leonardo designed engines of war for the duke of Milan, and later worked for Cesare Borgia in his campaign against cities of the Romagna.

Soldiers

Medieval armies consisted of the king's vassals and their own armed men, and local militias, conscripted peasants. Poor equipment and lack of training made them inefficient. Increasingly, armies were mostly mercenaries, men who fought for anyone who paid them. Of the army of 17,000 for the intended Spanish invasion of England in 1588, only 4,000 were Spaniards. Mercenaries were professionals, properly trained and owning their own equipment. But they were expensive, and sometimes unreliable. They sometimes became involved in politics. In Italy, several leaders of the mercenaries became rulers.

Below: These strange guns have several barrels and are fired from a stand. The lower one has a matchlock firing device, the other needs one man to aim and another to fire.

Firearms

Gunpowder, the first explosive, reached Europe from Islam in the 13th century. The first cannon was no more than a bronze tube, closed at one end, on a wooden mount, which fired a stone (later iron) ball. Cannons may have been used at the Battle of Crécy (1346) but they were generally only effective as siege weapons. Guns came later. A man had to carry a long, smouldering match to fire his *arquebus* gun and, as he also carried a bag of powder, he was prone to fatal accidents. His weapon was useless if it rained. The matchlock musket, invented in the late 16th century, could be aimed and was the first gun to have real influence on the battlefield.

An army with artillery and supplies on the way to battle. Gunpowder was milled with the machine on the left. Its ingredients were first mixed by hand and then pounded to fine grains. It was easy to make but needed care; one spark would cause an explosion.

Armor

Emperor Charles V had his first suit of fitted armor at the age of twelve. Full armor, made of hinged and shaped steel plates, reached its highest form around 1500. Charges by close-ranked mounted knights thundering into each other were no longer practicable (if they ever had been—English knights at the battle of Crécy got off their horses to fight). By 1600, full body armor had disappeared from war, though steel breastplates and helmets continued to be worn. The very heavy, decorated suits seen in museums today were probably worn mainly for jousts rather than battles.

Italian armor, about 1580, engraved and inlaid with gold and silver. This was for show, not for battle.

A matchlock musket with ivory decoration, made in Graz about 1570. It was not intended for war.

Armies and victims

Armies were growing larger, up to 40,000 men. Mercenary armies also had a greater number of camp followers, including their families. In general, they were expected to live off the land. Such vast numbers quickly stripped a region of food and, if discipline was poor, they also looted, raped, and murdered. When soldiers approached, peasants buried their valuables and fled to the nearest walled town. (Mercenaries did not like sieges, when hunger and disease killed more than any human enemy.) Things were worst in peace time, when unemployed mercenaries became bands of bandits.

Training a horse. An armored knight was very heavy, and medieval war horses were hefty like farm horses. In the 16th century, speedier horses were favored.

Cavalry

The striking arm of the medieval army was the cavalry, mounted knights in armor. Their charge was hard to resist and they could move quickly from place to place. But once knocked off his horse, the knight was helpless. Cavalry also needed space to manoeuvre, and dry ground. They were little used in the Netherlands, with its network of waterways. Infantry developed weapons to resist a cavalry charge—the pike or spear of Swiss mercenaries, over ten feet (3 m) long, and the *halberd*, a spear with a hook to pull a rider off his horse.

Fortifications

Cannon were most useful in sieges against castles and cities. The Turks captured Constantinople (1453), despite its massive walls, with guns so huge they had to be built on the site and never moved. During the French invasion of Italy, the artillery of Charles VIII reduced the fortress of San Giovanni in eight hours, though it had once withstood a siege for seven years. Military engineers adopted new plans against guns: lower profiles (high square towers were especially vulnerable), angled walls, earthworks that absorbed cannonballs, and of course their own guns.

Above: Forts on England's south coast built by Henry VIII (1509–1547) were small, low, and rounded so that cannonballs might be deflected.

The angled defence works of Castel Sant'Angelo, the pope's castle in Rome.

War and religion

One reason for the constant state of war was the lack of any international authority to check the aggression of national rulers. Although one medieval pope had tried to ban the crossbow, the Church was not against war on principle. The pope sometimes urged rulers to fight the Muslims rather than each other, but popes also took part in military alliances, and the clergy usually supported the ruler in his war aims. The Reformation made religion the cause of numerous wars and conflicts. It divided Europe into two camps led by Catholic Spain and Protestant England.

*Left: Machiavelli, author of a famous book on government (*The Prince*), was one of many writers on war.*

War at sea

Mediterranean warships were oared galleys, barely changed since ancient Rome, but with cannon in the bows. In the north, where sturdy square-sailed ships with no oars were the pattern, bow guns were useless unless the wind was behind. The answer was the "broadside," delivered sideways-on from cannon firing through ports in the ship's hull. The superiority of European ships and guns allowed the Portuguese to take over the Indian Ocean trade by force.

Left: The Mary Rose, Henry VIII's flagship (1512), may have been the first warship with batteries firing broadside.

The legendary St. Barbara, popular in the Middle Ages, who was imprisoned in a tower (her symbol) and became patron saint of sappers and gunners.

Renaissance Women

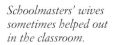

A woman's task in the 15th–16th century was to be a homemaker. She ran the household, supported her husband, who was her social superior, and looked after the children. Such an attitude was common in Europe until quite recent times. Independent women did exist, and they could be found in a variety of occupations, but they were exceptional. There were probably fewer women in 1600 than in 1450. Wives of soldiers or merchants had often stood in for their absent husbands, but mercenary armies and commercial agents made such absences less common. Few people, men or women, questioned the superiority of men. A Florentine writer, Vespasiano da Bisticci, said that women had two obligations: first, to bring up their children in the fear of God; second, to keep quiet in church—and preferably elsewhere. There were few male supporters of female independence.

Schoolmasters' wives sometimes helped out in the classroom.

Below: Margaret, favorite daughter and intellectual companion of Sir Thomas More (author of Utopia*), whose Latin works she translated into English after his death.*

Education

In noble families and a few wealthy middle-class families, girls as well as boys were often taught by private tutors, who were sometimes prominent scholars. Girls' schools for the well-off merchant class were run by nuns. But in general, the education of women was not taken seriously, and schooling was often interrupted by early marriage (a far more important matter at the time). As for the lower classes, education was regarded as pointless. Such girls needed only to learn the skills of housekeeping, from their mothers. But, due largely to the availability of printed books, more women were educated in the 16th century than earlier times.

A dowry chest was among the objects a bride brought to her new home.

Above: Lucrezia Borgia, who had three husbands: the Sforza lord of Pesaro (annuled by the pope, her father), a son of the king of Naples (murdered by her brother, Cesare), and the este duke of Ferrara.

Marriage as a business

Renaissance marriages were usually arranged for good business reasons. However, daughters had to be provided with a large dowry on marrying, which could almost bankrupt their family. Marriage was the best way for a ruler to extend his dominions (much cheaper than war, though almost as risky), for a landowner to increase his property, and for a banker to increase his wealth. Marriage alliances were a major topic of international diplomacy. The enormous personal empire of the Emperor Charles V was largely the result of the marriages arranged by Maximilian, his grandfather, for himself and his family.

Right: The birth of a baby was a time for celebration, and for relatives and friends to honor the mother.

Motherhood

The chief purpose of a family was to raise children. Although families were in general quite small, that was largely due to the high death rate of children. To raise two or three children to adulthood, a mother would have to give birth, on average, to eight or ten children. Girls usually married in their late teens, and as average life expectancy was only 35 to 40, married women might spend much of their adult life pregnant. Many died in childbirth, and the health of many more was harmed by so much child-bearing. For wealthy families, the strain of looking after children was reduced. Infants were often sent to a nurse, and in some regions young children were often lodged with some great household to be educated.

Working women

On farms and in lower-class trades such as shopkeeping, wives usually worked alongside their husbands. However, women were active independently in some other trades: they operated the ferries on the Rhône River, and were barbers in France. Dressmaking and embroidery depended entirely on female labor. In those cases, women were admitted to guilds, but they seldom rose to high office. A few women did hold important posts though. Susanne Erker was manager of the mint at Kutná Hora, near Prague. Anne of Brittany proved capable of ruling a country, Caterina Sforza of defending a city, and Elizabeth I was one of England's greatest monarchs.

Right: Women return from a day's work in the fields, from a painting by Brueghel.

Women and the Church

In the Middle Ages, the Church distrusted women because of their mysterious (sexual) power over men, and that attitude survived in the Renaissance. The best place for upper-class women who failed to find a husband, their fathers thought, was a convent (though not in Protestant countries). In a convent, their families would not have to support them. As nuns were usually educated women, some became scholars and intellectuals. An Italian nun, Beatrice del Sera, wrote a play that, though disguised as a religious drama, protests against confining women within the walls of a convent.

Nuns praying: many women became nuns not because their families forced them, but from religious conviction.

In congregations in early 15th-century Florence, the sexes were separated.

Women and art

For a woman to practice as an artist was difficult, and almost impossible in a city such as Florence. Of the small number of female artists who did achieve success, most were the daughters of artists and came from places more remote than Florence. Sofonisba Anguissola, perhaps the best known, was the highly educated daughter of a nobleman in Cremona, who encouraged her painting. Her work was praised by Michelangelo.

Above: Detail of a painting by Sofonisba Anguissola of herself and her sisters (also artists) playing chess.

Fashion

High fashion, for both men and women, reached exotic heights in the 15th century, with jewel-encrusted fabrics of astonishing richness, and colors to rival the feathers of tropical birds. In fashion as in art, Italy was the leader, though the popular slashing of garments to show streaks of contrasting color, seems to have begun, strangely, among Swiss soldiers. Women's costume generally exposed a lot of bosom but nothing else: skirts remained at floor length. Various governments passed sumptuary laws, forbidding people below a certain rank to wear certain clothes. The laws were generally ignored.

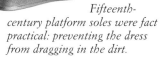

Fifteenth-century platform soles were fact practical: preventing the dress from dragging in the dirt.

Witches

Most people believed that witches—people, who had sold themselves to the devil—existed. What is surprising is that in the 16th–17th centuries, supposedly a more civilized time, the persecution of witches was greater than in the early Middle Ages. The victims were usually elderly, poor, lonely, and often feeble-minded women. They could be condemned on no more evidence than a complaint by a hostile neighbor. Since torture was widely used, they generally confessed. Some were persuaded to believe that they really were witches. People did protest against the persecution of witches, but few denied that witches existed (one who did was, amazingly, a courageous officer of the Spanish Inquisition).

Thousands of witches were executed in the 15th–16th centuries, usually by burning.

Women as patrons

Women from rich and courtly families often played an important cultural role. Ladies like Isabella d'Este and Elisabetta Gonzaga were partly responsible for the refined culture of courts such as Ferrara, Mantua, and Urbino. Isabella, who hired her own tutor to improve her Latin, was a zealous patron. She pursued artists she admired, like Leonardo and Giovanni Bellini, for years trying to persuade them to paint her a picture. Zoë Paleologus, wife of Ivan III, brought Italian Renaissance influence to Moscow. Lady Margaret Beaufort, mother of Henry VII, was a founder of two Cambridge colleges and patron of the first English printer, William Caxton.

Above: Isabella d'Este gave copies of this medallion of herself to poets she admired.

A cameo pendant, worn on the chest, with a scene of the birth of Jesus.

Piero di Cosimo's portrait of the beautiful Simonetta Vespucci. Her fashionably high forehead was achieved by shaving back the hairline.

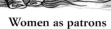
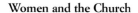

The World Beyond Europe

The period of the Renaissance was marked by growing contacts between Europe and the rest of the world. The period of rising nation states in Europe and the beginnings of overseas empires coincided with rise of three great Islamic empires. Of these, only the Ottoman Turkish empire (see pages 48–49) was directly involved in Europe. The smallest of the three was the Safavid empire of Persia (see page 49), and the most magnificent, the Mughal empire of India, whose achievements in the arts, especially architecture, equalled those of the European Renaissance. Further east, the Ming empire of China in the 15th century was still, in many ways, culturally more advanced than Europe. Japan was torn by civil war, but trade and culture were flourishing. In the Americas, the recently created empires of the Incas and Aztecs fell victim to superior European technology.

Headdress made of gold-studded feathers of the quetzal bird, given by Montezuma, the Aztec ruler, to the king of Spain in 1519.

The Aztecs

The Aztecs were the last of a series of dominant peoples through whom ancient Mexican culture was transmitted for many centuries. Their spectacular capital, Tenochtitlan, was a city of gardens, waterways, and immense buildings. Built on an island in a lake, it housed about 500,000 people. The Aztecs' subjects who, as in South America, belonged to many different groups with different languages, lived in villages and produced good crops of maize, although they had no plows, carts, or draft animals. The Aztecs were unpopular rulers. They imposed heavy taxes on their subjects, and their bloodthirsty gods demanded human sacrifices.

Figure of a god in gold and turquoise from the Chimú people of northern Peru, who were conquered by the Incas in 1476.

The mountain fortress-city of Machu Picchu was so remote that the Spaniards never discovered it in their 400-year rule.

The Incas

From about 1485, the Incas held sovereignty over most of South America west of the Andes, an empire of about 8 million people. The chief cities were built high in the Andes Mountains and were connected by good roads. Relay runners kept the rulers in touch with local affairs over huge distances and, in spite of the lack of a written language, this was in many ways a well-organized empire. For example, benefits were granted to the old and the sick. But it was no welfare state; the rulers, not their subjects, came first. All property officially belonged to the state, which dispersed land among the people.

NORTH AMERICA

ATLANTIC OCEAN

SOUTH AMERICA

Peru

Mansa Musa, pictured on a Catalan map of 1375, with a Tuareg, one of the nomadic raiders of the desert, whom he kept in check.

African empires

In the Middle Ages, a succession of powers arose in the western Sahel—the region between the Sahara Desert and the tropical forest. They controlled the valuable trade routes across the Sahara, bringing salt from the north and gold from the south. The Muslim rulers of Mali (larger than the modern state) in the 13th–14th centuries were both powerful and rich. Mansa Musa (1307–1332) distributed so much gold during his pilgrimage to Mecca (1324) that it affected prices in Europe. In the 15th century, Mali was superseded by the Songhai, former subjects, who were in turn defeated by the Moroccans in 1591.

African kingdoms

Another large state, Kanem-Bornu, lay to the east of Songhai. The kingdom of Benin, in what is now southern Nigeria, became famous for its metalwork and sculptures in bronze and ivory. At its height, under Oba (King) Equare in the late 15th century, it increased its territory through its powerful army, while profiting from trade in ivory, pepper, and slaves. Farther east lay the kingdom of Ethiopia, the one Christian country in Africa, whose Amhara kings claimed descent from the queen of Sheba and Solomon, king of Israel (recorded in the Old Testament and the Qur'an). Its rugged mountains protected it from the Muslim lowlands.

Bronze head of a queen, from Benin, 16th century.

Sonni Ali (reigned 1464–1492) made Songhai independent and captured Timbuktu (1469) and Djenne (1473), centers of trade and Muslim scholarship.

Wooden figure of a Luba prince who, having married a Lunda princess, founded a new kingdom farther south in what is now Angola.

Southern Africa

A number of kingdoms of Bantu-speaking people arose and fell in central parts of Africa. The Luba founded a kingdom on the Kasai River in the late 15th century, followed by the neighboring Lunda in the 16th century, who established a network of smaller, client kingdoms. In the southeast, the Rozwi (Mwena Mutapa) empire thrived on gold mined by female workers, and the Shona empire was based in the ancient capital of Great Zimbabwe. On the east coast several large, independent ports, generally ruled by Arabs, supplied African products to the flourishing Indian Ocean trade.

The Mughal empire

Babur, a Central Asian prince of part Mongol (Mughal) descent who had lost his lands, won a new kingdom farther south by defeating the Afghan ruler of Delhi at the battle of Panipat (1525). Under his grandson, Akbar (1555–1605), the Mughal empire included most of the Indian sub-continent. Akbar kept his empire through good government and tolerance, especially towards Hindus. At his court in Agra, he listened to devout Muslims, Hindus, and Christians (Jesuit missionaries), and contemplated a new religion based on the best of all three.

A Mughal artisan pounding paper in preparation for painting.

Above: Babur, from a Mughal miniature painted after his death. Like his descendants he was a cultured man, a poet, and author of fascinating memoirs.

Below: An elegant court building at Fatehpur Sikri.

Mughal art

Mughal style and culture, even cooking, astonished and fascinated every visitor. The main cultural influence was Persian, but it merged with other Muslim, as well as Hindu, traditions to develop its own unique character. Mughal painting, mainly miniatures (illustrations in manuscripts), was a court art, depending on the patronage of the emperor. Its subjects included historical events, such as Akbar's victories, hunting scenes, and court life.

Mughal miniature of Akbar attacking a Rajput fortress, which he won partly by force and partly by marrying a Rajput princess.

Fatehpur Sikri

More astonishing to the visitor than Mughal painting was Mughal architecture (it included perhaps the world's most beautiful building, the Taj Mahal, built by Akbar's grandson). In 1571–1585 Akbar built the magnificent ceremonial city of Fatehpur Sikri, near Agra, birthplace of Jahangir, his son and heir. Jahangir later described its numerous gardens, elegant edifices, pavilions, and other places of great beauty. Yet Akbar left it in 1585 and, except for one short visit, never returned. Fatehpur Sikri remained empty from then on.

EUROPE
ASIA
Japan
China
India
AFRICA
INDIAN OCEAN
AUSTRALIA

Left: Ming blue-and-white ware: Europeans could not get enough of this beautiful painted porcelain.

Chinese inventions

About 2,000 years ago, the Chinese first made porcelain—a hard, translucent pottery. Despite endless experiments, European potters discovered the secret less than 300 years ago. The long history of Chinese culture, based on the values taught by Confucius, helped the early development of science and technology. Among practical inventions that the Chinese made far ahead of Europeans were papermaking and printing, the seaman's compass, gunpowder, silk-making, clockwork, paper money, and the wheelbarrow (a boon to the peasants). But the Renaissance marks a turning point; from about 1500 Europe forged ahead.

Right: This clock tower was built in 1090.

Ming China

Under the strong and vigorous early rulers of the Ming dynasty (1368–1644), the Chinese empire was restored, and enjoyed 150 years of peace and prosperity. Irrigation works and new crop varieties produced more food, and life improved even for the hard-worked peasants. Economically, Ming China in the 15th century was ahead of Europe, where Chinese goods (tea, silk, porcelain) found a ready market. A new, wealthy merchant class developed, and Chinese ships—larger and safer than Europe's—ranged the Indian Ocean nearly 100 years before the Portuguese.

The Ming emperor Xuande (Hsüan-te, 1425–1435) was a responsible ruler who, himself a painter, encouraged the arts.

The German Jesuit, Schall von Bell, in Chinese costume. He was director of the observatory in Beijing.

Western visitors

The later Ming emperors did not like foreigners. Foreign travel and learning languages was forbidden. European traders, who arrived in the early 16th century, were unwelcome, though the Portuguese were allowed to settle in Macao (1557). One European visitor who was accepted, after long delays, was the Jesuit missionary Matteo Ricci (1552–1616), a well-educated man who adopted Chinese dress and customs and was eventually invited to the imperial court. He was followed by other scholarly men, speaking perfect Mandarin. One of them equipped the imperial army with modern artillery.

Mehmet II was a modernizer, who equipped his army with European guns and pursued a relentless policy of expansion.

Istanbul
The fall of Constantinople to the Ottoman Turks brought an end to the Christian empire of the east, which had lasted over 1,000 years. The last emperor, named Constantine like the first, died fighting, and Mehmet II, the conqueror, set up his throne in the church. The Turks had been at war with the Byzantines since the 7th century and had steadily whittled away at their empire over the centuries. The Ottoman sultans needed Constantinople in order to unite their Asian and European possessions and extend their conquests beyond the Balkans. Renamed Istanbul, it became the Ottoman capital.

Above: In 1453 the Church of the Holy Wisdom, for centuries the greatest church in Europe, became a mosque (from a 16th-century painting).

Suleiman the Magnificent
In the short, eventful reign of Selim I, the Ottoman empire became larger and richer. Under Selim's son, Ottoman power and wealth reached its peak. Suleiman I (1520–66) was called the Magnificent by Europeans impressed by the splendor of his court, but his own people called him the Law-giver. His government was fair and efficient, his subjects well-fed and reasonably contented, but Suleiman was above all a great war leader, like his father. His armies marched deep into central Europe, and the capture of the island-fortress of Rhodes from the Christian Knights of St John gave the Ottoman navy the key to the eastern Mediterranean.

The Ottoman Empire

After the destruction of the Seljuk Turks by the Mongols in 1243, the Ottomans, gained power in Anatolia (modern-day Turkey). They rapidly increased their territory, mainly at the expense of the Byzantine empire, and in 1453 they conquered Constantinople (Istanbul), after carrying 70 ships overland to launch them in the rear of the Byzantine fleet. They became an increasingly serious threat to Europe. Several popes tried to organize new crusades against them, but this was no longer practical politics because the European states were busy fighting each other. Under Sultan Selim I (1512–1520), the Ottomans added Egypt, Syria, and part of Safavid Persia to their empire. They conquered Hungary in 1526 and besieged Vienna in 1529. After capturing Rhodes (1522), they challenged the Christians for control of the Mediterranean. Under the great Suleiman (1520–1566), the Ottoman empire stretched from the borders of Austria to Morocco, the Yemen (southern Arabia), and Persia (Iran).

Left: Painting from the Topkapi Museum of the Ottoman siege of Vienna (1529). It began too late in the year. Autumn gales, Danube floods, and illness made Suleiman withdraw.

Right: One of the courts of the Topkapi palace. The Gate of Felicity (top right) led to the Sultan's private apartments.

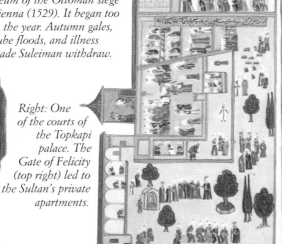

The Sultan's palace
The Topkapi Saray (then a palace, today a museum) in Istanbul was sited on a small peninsula, surrounded by the sea. It is more like a town than a European palace and today has over 100 separate buildings. Besides the numerous personnel and paraphernalia of the imperial court, it included the main departments of government, many military units, schools, hospitals, lawyers, scholars, poets, and the extensive private quarters of the women (the harem). Most of these people—up to 5,000 in all—were, technically, slaves.

Below: The janissaries were subject only to the sultan and their own officers.

The Ottoman army
The chief reason for the success of the Sultan's forces was the world's first professional army, the *janissaries*. Most of them came from Christian peasant families, taken as boys to Istanbul and educated as Turkish-speaking Muslim soldiers (others entered the civil service). They lived by their own strict rules, in their own quarters (they could not marry), and were intensely loyal to the sultan, who gave them special privileges. The Ottoman army was also well supplied with guns. Its conquests in the west were limited only by the long line of communications from Istanbul and the need to remain prepared for trouble from the Safavids in the east.

The Ottoman Empire
conquests ▢ 1492 ▢ 1566
▢ 1520 ▢ 1640

Although some provinces were added later, the Ottoman empire was never again so powerful as in the reign of Suleiman I.

The Ottoman navy

The great Islamic powers usually lacked a navy to match their armies. But the expanding Ottoman empire needed a navy to defend its coasts from Christian attacks. Ships played a part in a war against Venice (1499–1503), but a more formidable fleet of war galleys was created by Suleiman I's admiral Kheir-ed-din (Barbarossa). He was a successful North African corsair, who won a famous victory over the Habsburg admiral, Andrea Doria, at Prevesa in 1538. The tables were turned at Lepanto (1571) when several Christian states for once combined, and destroyed the lighter Ottoman galleys (they were soon rebuilt though).

The decisive Ottoman victory at Chaldiran (1514) checked Safavid advances in eastern Anatolia.

Lepanto was the last great battle between galleys, vessels driven by oars and armed with a ram.

Ottoman society

The Ottoman empire was a multinational state, and a very successful one. Although women played little part, and did not even socialize with men, in other respects Ottoman rule was, by European standards, liberal—less biased against Christians than Christians were against Muslims. Many of the sultan's subjects were Christians, and in general, men of Christian origin were preferred to Turks in government posts. Most officials, even the grand vizier (chief minister), were non-Turkish. Those who had been officials under Byzantine rule often stayed at their post under the Ottomans. A man rose in public service on merit, not through birthrite.

Above: Millers grinding grain with a mobile, horse-powered mill.

The Arts

The colorful, often floral-patterned pottery named after the town of Iznik (Nicea), whose colors included a unique, brilliant red that no imitator could reproduce, is regarded as the finest 16th-century pottery in Islam. Ottoman court painting approached the more renowned Persian art, which strongly influenced Mughal painters. The most spectacular achievement in Ottoman arts is the plan of the domed mosque, associated with the great architect Sinan. The best remaining examples of Safavid architecture are from the 17th century, when Shah Abbas built his magnificent capital of Isfahan.

Above: A procession of the guilds, late 16th century: every occupation had its own guild, or brotherhood.

Safavid Iran

In 1502 a rival to the Ottoman empire appeared when another Turkish dynasty, the Safavids, established themselves in Iran. The Ottomans were orthodox Sunni Muslims, whose sultan claimed the authority of caliph over all Islam, but the Safavids were Shi'ite, and had many supporters among the tribes of eastern Anatolia. The result was continual conflict. The Safavid empire peaked in the reign of Abbas the Great (1586–1628). He regained all the land lost to the Ottomans in earlier wars and captured Baghdad, victories that united the Iranian peoples as one nation and encouraged Persian industry and arts.

Carpets

The ancient art of carpet-making, which was practiced by nomads in ancient times, flourished in both Islamic empires. The best-known type is the prayer rug, especially from Anatolia, which generally represents the mihrab (prayer niche) of a mosque. They were made on simple hand looms, easily transported. Carpets were hand-knotted, usually in wool (silk for the finest), and Turks and Persians used different types of knot. The finest court carpets contained hundreds of knots per square inch. Dyes were derived mainly from plants. Experienced dyers were said to be able to produce 100 different shades of red.

Above: Iznik pottery, tin-glazed earthenware (faience).

Left: This ceramic mosque lamp was made during the reign of Suleiman the Magnificent.

A prayer rug from Hereke, the Ottoman court workshops near Istanbul, which followed the Persian rather than the native Turkish style.

49

Voyages of Discovery

Europe's vital trade with the East was threatened by the dominance of the Ottoman empire in the eastern Mediterranean. At the same time, Europeans began to consider the possibility of opening a trade route direct to Asia by sea, bypassing the Mediterranean and cutting out all the middlemen who controlled Asian trade. European ships in the 15th century, although they had never sailed far from land, were capable of long voyages. Educated people knew that the Earth is round, and they believed it was much smaller than it is. Columbus and others calculated that by sailing west across the Atlantic they would reach the eastern shores of Japan and China. No one knew that a vast double continent—the Americas—lay in between, or that another ocean, even wider than the Atlantic, lay beyond that. Others, knowing nothing of Africa beyond Morocco, wondered if they could sail around Africa to the East.

A Portuguese map of Africa and the Indian Ocean made in 1558.

Vasco da Gama led the first Portuguese expedition to the east African ports and India (1497–1498).

An astrolabe measured the height of a heavenly body in degrees above the horizon. But the movement of the sea made accurate measurements difficult.

The art of navigation

To navigate, a sea captain relied, first, on the stars, chiefly the sun and, at night, on the Pole Star, which always marks north. He could calculate his latitude (distance north–south) by measuring the height of the sun or Pole Star above the horizon. He had a compass, but he did not know a compass indicates magnetic north, not true north. He had no way of measuring distance traveled except by intelligent guesswork, and, worst of all, no means of measuring longitude (distance east–west).

Above: Images of Genoa (left) and Venice (right), from a 14th-century chart. In 1380 Genoa was decisively defeated by Venice.

The spice trade

The Eastern trade was small but very valuable. It included spices, such as pepper, cloves, ginger, and nutmeg, but also things like sugar, silk, and dyes. These reached the Mediterranean via the Red Sea or Persian Gulf, or overland across central Asia. Traditionally, the European end of the trade was largely controlled by Genoa and Venice, but Ottoman conquests interrupted the old trade routes.

Sugar cane remained a luxury in Europe until bulk cargoes came from Asia and the Caribbean in the 16th century.

The Portuguese in India

In 1487, Portuguese captain Bartolomeu Dias ventured past the Cape of Good Hope, the southern tip of Africa, into the Indian Ocean. Voyages to India followed. With superior guns and ships, the Portuguese took over the Indian Ocean trade by force. Afonso Albuquerque, Governor-general of Portuguese India in 1509–1515, seized Malacca, the key to the East Indies (modern Indonesia), establishing Portuguese posts as far east as the Moluccas, the fabled Spice Islands.

Columbus

Christopher Columbus, a Genoese captain, gained Spanish support to seek a westward route to Asia. With three small ships he sailed from Seville in 1492. Six weeks' sailing brought him to islands that he believed were the East Indies (they are still called the West Indies). Soon hundreds of Spaniards, hoping to find gold and make a fortune, followed him to what proved to be a new continent. Unlike Asia, the Americas were thinly populated by people who had little resistance to European technology and aggression.

Left: Columbus made four voyages to America, but never admitted that it was not Asia.

Dividing the world

Spain and Portugal disputed rights to the newly discovered lands (they did not consider that the lands belonged to their non-Christian inhabitants). The pope was called in to arbitrate, and the final settlement was made in the Treaty of Tordesillas (1494). A line was drawn through the middle of the Atlantic. West of the line was Spanish, east of it Portuguese. However, other up-and-coming sea powers, especially the English and French, rejected this division of the world.

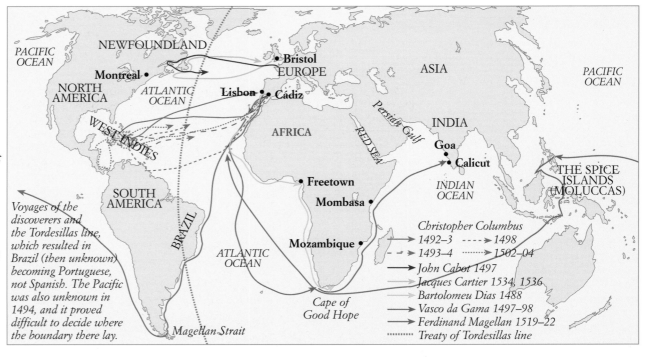

Voyages of the discoverers and the Tordesillas line, which resulted in Brazil (then unknown) becoming Portuguese, not Spanish. The Pacific was also unknown in 1494, and it proved difficult to decide where the boundary there lay.

Christopher Columbus
→ 1492–3 ----→ 1498
--→ 1493–4 →1502–04
→ John Cabot 1497
→ Jacques Cartier 1534, 1536
→ Bartolomeu Dias 1488
→ Vasco da Gama 1497–98
→ Ferdinand Magellan 1519–22
········· Treaty of Tordesillas line

Around the world

Ferdinand Magellan, a Portuguese working for Spain, hoped to find a route to the East via a strait through the Americas. He sailed in 1519, with five ships, but discovered that the only strait lay near the tip of South America. The vast width of the Pacific was another setback. He made it eventually, but was killed in the Philippines. One of his ships, the Vittoria, sailed on, under Sebastian del Cano, across the Indian Ocean and around the Cape, reaching Seville after 37 months. Only 18 out of 260 men who started, returned to tell of their voyage around the world.

Right: Magellan fires a salute as he leaves Seville.

Map making

European knowledge of geography in the 15th century was based on the work of Ptolemy, who lived in the 2nd century. Medieval maps were just beautiful pictures, and practical marine charts made for sailors followed principles that made them highly inaccurate over a large area. Any flat map of the world is bound to be distorted. What Renaissance navigators needed was a method of projection in which the distortion was consistent, so the navigator could make allowances for it. This was not achieved until 1569 when Mercator (Gerhard Kremer) produced his world atlas on the projection named after him.

English and French discoverers

The first European to reach North America since the long-forgotten Vikings was John Cabot, Italian-born but serving the king of England. He discovered the rich fishery off Newfoundland, but apart from fish, the region seemed unattractive. In 1534 Jacques Cartier explored the Gulf of St. Lawrence for France. On a second voyage he reached the future Quebec and Montreal. The first European colonies in North America—the English in Virginia, the French in Quebec—were founded in the early 17th century.

Left: Cartier, like most others in North America, was interested in a sea route to the East, not in colonies.

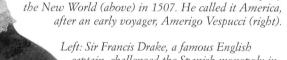

Martin Waldseemuller made one of the earliest maps of the New World (above) in 1507. He called it America, after an early voyager, Amerigo Vespucci (right).

Left: Sir Francis Drake, a famous English captain, challenged the Spanish monopoly in the Americas and visited northern California on a voyage around the world (1577–1580).

The capture of Mexico

Rumors of a wealthy kingdom in Mexico reached the Spaniards in Cuba, and in 1517 Hernan Cortés led an expedition to Vera Cruz. On arriving he burned his ships; there could be no retreat. He made allies of the subject peoples of the Aztecs and marched on Tenochtitlan. The Spaniards were admitted to the island city by Montezuma, the Aztec emperor, but after an uneasy interlude, trouble broke out, the Spaniards captured the city, and the whole Aztec empire soon fell into their hands.

Left: After the fall of the Aztecs, Cortés became ruler of New Spain, a region larger than Spain itself.

Right: The El Dorado legend was probably based on a custom of an earlier age, when a king was anointed with gold dust (imagined by Théodore de Bry, 1590).

The search for El Dorado

The Spanish adventurers who flocked to the New World were besotted by dreams of gold. Among the stories that excited them was the legend of a golden king, El Dorado, who threw gold and jewels into Lake Guatavita as an offering. The Spaniards tried to drain the lake of gold, and did find a little, but the real riches lay not in legends of treasure but in real mines, like Potosí in Bolivia, which provided the silver that annual treasure fleets carried to Spain.

An ivory carving from Benin shows a Portuguese slave-trading expedition.

South America

The other great American empire, the Inca empire of Peru, was weakened by civil conflict when Francisco Pizarro, an uneducated adventurer, arrived with only 180 men in 1531. By treachery, the Spaniards killed the emperor, Atahualpa, and in a few years, took over the Inca empire. Many Spanish conquistadors, like Pizarro, were brutal men, who killed and enslaved thousands of people. But the worst killers were European diseases, which wiped out whole populations.

The regal figure of Atahualpa, last of the Incas. Captured by Pizarro's men, he offered a roomful of gold treasures as ransom, but was murdered anyway.

Right: Las Casas, called the "Apostle" in the Indies, was supported by the government in his efforts to end the Encomienda system of forced labor.

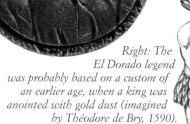

The slave trade

Spaniards forced the native people in America to work in their fields and mines. Many died from exhaustion and cruel treatment, or from diseases like smallpox that they had no immunity against. The Spaniards needed tougher laborers, and found them in Africa. The first slave auction of captured Africans took place in Portugal in 1444. The demand for labor in the Americas encouraged the growth of the Atlantic slave trade, a shameful episode in European history that lasted nearly 400 years.

Missionaries

Besides trying to convert American slaves to Christianity, Roman Catholic missionaries tried to protect the slaves from the worst atrocities. The Dominican priest Bartolomé de Las Casas (1474–1566) spent a lifetime trying to improve their conditions, against fierce opposition. His *History of the Indies* revealed their sufferings at the hands of his countrymen.

The Hussites

Though a small nation, the Czechs have often had a powerful impact on European history, especially in the Hussite wars. Jan Hus was a religious reformer a century before the Reformation. His execution by the Church fired his followers to launch a war against the Habsburg emperor (who was also king of Bohemia). They had support from the Czech nobles (some perhaps hoping to gain Church property), and were inspired not only by religious zeal but also by Czech nationalism and hostility to German influence in the Czech lands. The revolt of the Hussites, though eventually defeated, was echoed in the Reformation and later European conflicts.

Hus was condemned by a council of the Church and burned as a heretic in 1415.

Ingenious portrait of a vegetable man, by Giuseppe Arcimboldo, an Italian painter who settled in Rudolph II's Prague.

Bohemia

The intellectual, Czech-speaking Emperor Charles IV, who was also king of Bohemia (1346–1378), made Prague his capital. It became culturally the liveliest city in Europe under his wise and capable rule. Hradcany Castle, Charles Bridge, and the University (the first in the Holy Roman Empire) are among his memorials. The Czech Lands were almost ruined by the Hussite wars, but in the late 16th century, life improved under Habsburg emperors such as the scholarly Rudolph II (1576–1612).

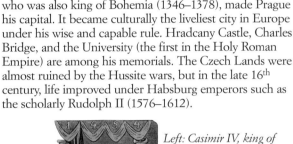

Left: Casimir IV, king of Poland (1447–1492), gained land from the old rival rulers of Lithuania, the Teutonic Knights.

Eastern Europe

With some exceptions, in about 1500, eastern Europe was more backward than the west. Though it contained large states, royal government was weak, largely because most kings were elected. That led to crisis when a ruler died. Selfish and lawless nobles preferred, if possible, a weak candidate who would not stop them from acting just as they pleased. Poland, the largest kingdom in Europe, would later be reduced to anarchy by its lack of a strong monarchy. Peace and stability were further disrupted by the religious Reformation, local wars, and the advance of the Ottoman Turks. In western Europe, ordinary people were gaining more freedom and towns were growing richer, but in the east the opposite was happening. Serfdom, a modified form of slavery, was quickly disappearing in the west by 1500, but was increasing in Russia. However, there were bright spots. Cities like Prague or Cracow enjoyed a cultural golden age, but it was short.

The Jagiellon dynasty

Jagiello, grand duke of Lithuania, became king of Poland in 1386, creating a huge state. In the late 15th century, a junior branch of the dynasty became kings of Bohemia and Hungary. Although they ruled like hereditary monarchs, the Jagiellon kings never managed to abolish the principle of royal election. The Polish nobles, growing rich on grain exports from their large estates, enjoyed extensive liberties and prevented the development of strong central government. The line ended with the death of Sigismund II of Poland in 1572.

In this early 16th-century book, the king is pictured with the Sejm, the Polish lawmaking assembly.

The Renaissance in Poland

Cracow, the Polish capital, where the first printing press opened in 1473, was a major center of humanism. The Jagiellons attracted Italian artists, scholars and architects to their court. One of Europe's finest late Gothic sculptors, the German Veit Stoss, settled in Cracow. Many Polish students went to Italian universities. Cracow university itself had 15,000 students, among them Copernicus, the first to prove that the Earth revolves around the Sun. Poland itself produced notable painters.

Carved wooden figure from the church of St. Mary in Cracow, the masterpiece of Veit Stoss (died 1553).

Lands ruled by members of the Jagiellon dynasty about 1500.

The Vasa dynasty

The rising power in northeast Europe in the 16th century was newly independent Sweden, under the Vasa dynasty (1523–1818). In 1592 King Sigismund III Vasa, who was a grandson of a Jagiellon king of Poland, succeeded his uncle, Stephen Bathory, as king of Poland, thus uniting the two dynasties. But his hostility to Lutheranism in Sweden led to civil war and his overthrow (1599) by Charles IX. In Poland, civil war further reduced the authority of the monarchy. However, Vasa's son, Wladyslaw IV, succeeded him as king.

Left: Gustavus Vasa was elected king of Sweden in 1523.

Anna, a sister of the last Jagiellion king, became queen by her marriage to Stephen Bathory (reigned 1575–1586).

The Tsars

The grand duke Ivan III of Muscovy (Moscow), united the Russian lands under his rule (1462–1505) and freed them from domination by the Tatars. He first used the title "tsar" (emperor), officially adopted by his grandson, Ivan IV (1533–1584). Ivan IV strengthened the Crown, bringing the nobles to order and reforming government and the law. Abroad, he opened trade with Western Europe, and took Kazan and Astrakhan from the Tatars. That gave Russia access to the Caspian Sea, but Ivan's war with Poland-Lithuania failed to gain Russian access to the Baltic. The death in 1560 of his much-loved first wife, Anastasia Romanov, soured Ivan, whose failures and brutalities in his later years earned him the nickname "the Terrible."

Ivan IV, an able ruler as a young man, a brutal tyrant in later years.

The Kremlin (citadel) of Moscow in the late 16th century. Much of it was built by Italians invited to Moscow by Ivan III.

The Russian Cap of State, a symbol of royal authority, was originally worn by an 11th century prince of Kiev and inherited by the Russian tsars.

The boyars

The boyars, the landowning Russian nobility, represented a threat to the personal authority of the grand dukes and tsars. Many of them lived in Moscow, where their plots and quarrels dominated the throne during the childhood of Ivan IV (who inherited the title at age three). Ivan, always a violent man, turned on the boyars after 1560, blaming them for Anastasia's death. A reign of terror followed. Hundreds of boyars were killed, some fled abroad and others were ruined by Ivan's punishing reforms.

Left: In spite of Ivan's persecution, the boyars survived as a class, though they lost their independence and depended on the favor of the Tsar.

The peasants

A Russian peasant. The descent of a free peasant into serfdom, a condition little different from slavery, was partly the result of state policy.

Ivan IV's campaign against the boyars brought trouble to the countryside, and many great estates were broken up. The peasants were freed from obligations to their former landlords, but they had nowhere to go. Many became homeless, some became colonists in the frontier regions, and some joined the Cossack outlaws. A huge amount of farm land was abandoned. Since peasant labor was necessary for food production, Ivan made a law depriving them of their right to move. Thus, the great mass of the Russian peasants, who were, legally, free tenants in 1500, by 1600 became serfs—the subjects of their landlords.

Right: The expansion of Russia in the 15th century was the beginning of a long process that would result in an empire stretching from the Baltic to the Pacific.

BARENTS SEA

SWEDEN

NOVGOROD

LITHUANIA

Moscow

KHANATE OF KAZAN

KHANATE OF CRIMEA

Muscovite territory
- end of 13th century
- acquisitions to 1462
- acquisitions under Ivan III

Russian art

Art in Russia was almost exclusively religious. Although Ivan III imported Italian artists in the final phase of the rebuilding of the Kremlin, the Renaissance had little effect in Russia. The Byzantine influence dominated art and architecture until interrupted by the Mongol conquest (13th–15th centuries). Isolation encouraged the development of a national style, in which, by the 15th century, the icon (religious image) became the leading form of art in the work of artists such as Rublev and Dionysius. Architecture, traditionally in wood, was typified by tall churches with multiple onion-shaped domes, cone-like towers, drums, and gables, richly decorated with tall, jewel-like altar screens.

Gilded and jeweled icon of St. Nicholas, patron saint of Russia, made in a Moscow Kremlin workshop under Ivan IV.

Left: The church of St. Basil in Moscow (begun 1554) commemorated Ivan IV's conquests against the Tatars.

Religion

The most important result of Byzantine influence was religious. Russia was converted to Greek Orthodox Christianity before 1000. After the fall of Constantinople (1453), leadership of the Eastern Church passed to the fast-growing power of Moscow. When Ivan IV adopted the title "tsar," he proclaimed himself the successor to the Byzantine emperors, the guardians of Orthodoxy. Although it held vast estates, and its leader, the Metropolitan Macarius, strongly influenced his pupil Ivan IV. The Russian Church was dependent on the government, unlike the Roman Church.

After a period of political upheaval following Ivan IV's death, Mikhail Romanov established his dynasty that ruled 304 years.

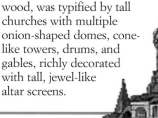

Science and Superstition

Knowledge made rapid advances during the Renaissance, due in part to printed books. The recovery of the works of the ancient thinkers and the growth of humanism created the conditions for a spirit of scientific inquiry. Early humanists treated the works of the ancients with respect and reverence, almost as Christians treated the Bible. But soon their studies led them to question even some statements of the ancients, and they began to make their own discoveries about the world. True science was beginning (though it was not called science, then). As people's knowledge and abilities grew, new activities became possible, such as ocean voyaging, which introduced Europeans to new lands and peoples. These exciting advances had little effect on most ordinary people. By the 16th century, science still had less influence than superstition.

Chart grading the colors of urine, which was believed to indicate the ailment the patient was suffering from.

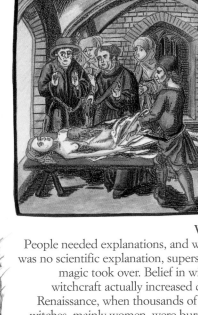

Ivory figure, made after Vesalius, which demonstrates the organs of the body.

Medicine

Physicians had few weapons against disease or serious injury. Medicine was still largely a mixture of magic spells and common sense, though many herbs were used (and some were effective). The Swiss Paracelsus recommended laudanum (opium) as a sedative. Everyone understood the dangers of infection—that the best way to avoid plague was to flee the area—but not its cause. Some wise physicians recommended fresh air, exercise, and a healthy diet, as they do today.

Left and below: The basis of medicine was the works of ancient Greeks. These illustrations of how to bandage head and leg wounds were based on a 2nd century physician.

Anatomy

Though he never dissected a human body, the great authority on human anatomy was Galen, who died in 200 A.D. In 1543 his authority was surpassed by *The Fabric of the Human Body*, by Andreas Vesalius. With clear and beautiful illustrations, it corrected many of Galen's mistakes. Vesalius taught at Padua, which became Europe's leading medical school.

Alchemy

Alchemy was chemistry before science. Alchemists were usually learned men who based their ideas on ancient authorities, but with a strong element of magic and mysticism. The chief aim of alchemists was to find the "Philosopher's Stone." There were many reasons for pursuing this mysterious substance, including the belief that it would make the old young again and would turn ordinary metal into gold.

Left: A crab, relief sculpture from a series illustrating the signs of the zodiac.

Above: An alchemist directs his assistants.

Left: A page from a French encyclopedia of 1486. Drawings could be printed as easily as text, but color was added by hand.

Right: Dissection shows that this dead witch has a toad in place of a heart, proof that she is a creature of the devil!

Recording nature

The invention of printing opened up new opportunities for illustrators as well as writers. Earlier, manuscripts had been illustrated by hand—a long, laborious job. Printed books contained illustrations called wood cuts, with the design cut in a block of hard wood, which could be combined with metal type in printing a complete page.

Right: The accuracy of artists in representing plants, here in a painting by Dürer, was displayed in many books on herbs and medicines.

Witchcraft

People needed explanations, and when there was no scientific explanation, superstition and magic took over. Belief in witches and witchcraft actually increased during the Renaissance, when thousands of supposed witches, mainly women, were burned. Most confessed—not surprising as they were tortured until they did. As a brave Spaniard said, the trouble was not witches but the campaigns against them. They were neither witches nor bewitched until they were talked about.

Keeping time

The first mechanical clocks appeared around 1300, usually in the old bell towers of churches. Driven by weights, they rang a bell. Until then it had been done by a bell ringer. Early clocks were made by blacksmiths and had no dial. In the Renaissance, a variety of clocks, including domestic clocks and portable clocks (about 1500), or watches, came into use. They were driven by a spring, a revolution in clock-making.

Left: In the 16th century, clocks became ornaments as well as timekeepers.

Musical instruments

A much greater variety of music was written in the Renaissance. Opera began before 1600. Musical instruments were costly, but wealthy families owned traditional instruments such as the lute (plucked like a harp) and viol (ancestor of the violin). A big innovation was the development of the harpsichord family, keyboard instruments in which the strings are mechanically plucked (not struck as in a piano).

Left: an early copy of Copernicus' book, On the Revolution of Heavenly Bodies.

Left: An armillary sphere. The astronomer Tycho Brahe (1546–1601) devised new types. This one shows features of the Earth (equator, tropics, etc.)

Right: This instrument was used for calculating heights and distances, by architects as well as surveyors.

Astronomy

Astronomy could be considered the most exciting study in Renaissance science. In 1543 Copernicus, a Polish-born monk, allowed his book about the universe, which suggested that the earth moved around the sun, to be published. He had written it years before, on the basis of mathematical calculations, but would not publish it earlier because it contradicted Ptolemy and the teaching of the Church. When he was dying, he allowed it to be published.

Right: Nearly 100 years after Copernicus, the Church forbade Galileo (who, unlike Copernicus, had a telescope), to teach the Copernican theory of a Sun-centered solar system.

Water power

The main sources of mechanical power were wind and water. Water mills, which harnessed the power of river currents, dated from ancient times. Windmills, especially useful in the Low Countries where rivers moved slowly, were rare until the 14th century. The earliest were post mills, in which the whole body of the mill could be moved to face the wind. Tower mills, in which only the cap carrying the sails moved, appeared during the Renaissance.

Right: Mills could be used to pump water from mines. This one from 1580 raised water to work a fountain.

Left: Among the smaller instruments in the harpsichord family was the virginal.

Mathematics

The main tool of science was mathematics, which included a variety of subjects: arithmetic, geometry, astronomy, astrology, music, military strategy, and navigation. This was a major subject of education, equally important for the shopkeeper and the artist. (Leonardo said an artist must know his math, and Dürer published a book on mathematics). Arabic numbers replaced the clumsy Roman numerals, and decimals and logarithms were introduced.

Right: Raphael's famous fresco The School of Athens *portrayed ancient Greek scholars, including Pythagoras and Euclid, pioneers of geometry.*

Measuring distances

In ancient times, distances were measured by men trained to walk at an exact pace. In the Renaissance, surveyors used triangulation. which meant taking bearings on two high points (such as a church steeple or a hilltop) from a third. Measuring wheels established the exact distance between points, necessary to measure the distance of roads or rivers, not traveling in a straight line.

Mapmaking

Medieval maps were religious pictures, not useful for finding your way around. The beginning of modern mapmaking began with the study of Ptolemy, the great Greek geographer of the 2nd century A.D. Maps that used new mathematical projections that allowed for the curve of the Earth's surface and benefitted from the voyages of discovery gave people their first understanding of geography – of how the Earth actually is.

This globe, made in 1492, gives a fairly accurate picture of Europe and the west coast of Africa as far as the Cape of Good Hope—the farthest point then reached by Europeans.

England and Scotland

The Renaissance reached Britain late. England's cultural golden age did not peak until the last twenty years of the reign of Elizabeth I (1558–1603), and it was largely reflected in literature, especially plays and poetry, and in music, rather than the visual arts. Politically, however, England was ahead of most other European countries, with a stable national state under a strong monarchy. In Scotland, though little touched by Italian influence, learning and the arts flourished in the reign of the cultured James IV (1488–1513), a rare period of peace. James married an English princess, but the old hostility between Scots and English soon resumed when Henry VIII revived English ambitions to control Scotland. The two kingdoms both became Protestant, though of different types, and in 1603 the King of Scots peacefully inherited the English Crown.

An attack on a town during the Wars of the Roses. There were few big battles, and casualties outside the nobility were small.

Right: The Scottish crown, remodeled for James V in 1540 but originally much older.

Henry VII encouraged trade, avoided war, and employed zealous tax collectors: he was respected but not loved.

The Wars of the Roses

From 1455, England was afflicted by civil wars arising from a contest for the Crown between rival royal families, the Houses of York (its badge a white rose) and Lancaster (a red rose). The wars ended in 1485 with the victory of Henry Tudor (Henry VII, 1485–1509), a Lancastrian who ended the rivalry by marrying a Yorkist queen and establishing a strong, prosperous kingdom. Henry VII was one of the few Renaissance rulers who kept his spending below his income. Although the Wars of the Roses had thinned out the ranks of the nobles, they had not seriously damaged the economy.

The Stewarts

The Stewart dynasty ruled Scotland for nearly 350 years, but few of those years were peaceful, and before 1600, few kings died in their bed. As a result, many succeeded when still children, a regent governed for them, allowing the unruly Scottish nobles to pursue their own ambitions. Border raids kept Scots and English busy, and much of the Highlands were barely under royal control. The interval of peace and good government under James IV ended with an English invasion and the massacre of Scottish leaders, including James, at the battle of Flodden (1513). James V reasserted Scottish independence but was himself defeated in 1542.

Henry VII
(reigned 1485–1509)

Margaret Tudor, wife of James IV of Scots

Catherine of Aragon, first wife of Henry VIII

Anne Boleyn, second wife of Henry VIII

Jane Seymour, third wife of Henry VIII

James V
(reigned 1513–1542)

Henry VIII
(reigned 1509–1547)

Mary, queen of Scots
(reigned 1542–1567)

James VI of Scotland
(reigned 1567–1625),
became James I of England
(reigned 1603–1625)

Mary I
(reigned 1553–1558)

Elizabeth I
(reigned 1558–1603)

Edward VI
(reigned 1547–1553)

The Tudors

The Tudor dynasty reigned for 118 years but included only three generations: Henry VII, his son Henry VIII, and Henry VIII's three children, who all died childless. Henry VIII, whose efforts to gain a male heir resulted in his six marriages, was responsible for creating the Church of England, with himself at its head. It remained Catholic in belief and worship until it adopted a Protestant system under Edward VI. Edward's early death resulted in the succession of his older sisters, Mary, a devout Catholic who restored the Church of Rome, and Elizabeth, who reestablished a Church of England with a moderately Protestant form of worship. Elizabeth was the most popular of all English monarchs, treated by poets as a goddess. Her reign is seen as England's most glorious, but failure to reform government finances stored up trouble for the future.

The Reformation

Henry VIII was a poor governor but a formidable personality. He ended the pope's authority out of resentment (the pope refused to give him a divorce), but the result was a stronger national kingdom and greater authority for Parliament (not something Henry intended). He inherited a full treasury but squandered it in extravagant displays and pointless expeditions against the French and Scots. Elizabeth was more intelligent and a wiser ruler. She employed excellent ministers, tried to avoid war, and presided over a final settlement of the Church of England. Her decision not to marry was clever diplomacy—it kept foreign rulers guessing—and besides, a king would have reduced her power. Well-educated, she encouraged the arts and literature.

Sir Thomas More (1477–1535), English scholar (author of Utopia) *and Lord Chancellor, executed for opposing Henry's takeover of the English Church.*

Right: Of the 130 ships of the Armada, only half returned to Spain. The war continued until 1604.

This map shows the sites of major battles of the Wars of the Roses (1455–1487).

King's College Chapel, Cambridge, completed 1515. It was both an engineering masterpiece and a supreme example of the beautiful English late-Gothic style.

England and Spain

Under Elizabeth, England became the leading Protestant nation in Europe, with a powerful navy—and thus the enemy of mighty Spain. England supported the Protestant Dutch in their revolt against Spanish rule, while launching piratical raids on Spain's colonial American empire. The Spanish King Philip II (who had been briefly married to Elizabeth's Catholic sister Mary) finally lost patience. In 1588 he launched a powerful invasion fleet, known to the English as the Spanish Armada. Dogged by bad weather and the smaller but nimbler English ships, it failed.

Mary, queen of Scots

Mary was sent to France in 1547, at age five, to marry the future king, who died in 1559. She returned to Scotland as queen, essentially French, and a Catholic, in a country dominated by the anti-Catholic, anti-French party. Her romantic marriage to a cousin, Lord Darnley, was a disaster, and Mary perhaps encouraged Darnley's murder. Soon after, she married Thomas Bothwell, a Protestant but a rogue. The Scottish lords rebelled, and Mary was defeated and fled to England. She had a claim to the English throne, supported by Spain and other Catholic interests. Her involvement in plots against Elizabeth I led to her execution in 1587.

Mary's rosary and prayer book. Her own actions were the main cause of her troubles.

Humanism

The chief centers of learning were Oxford and Cambridge universities, where Italian humanists taught in the 15th century. English champions of the New Learning included John Colet, Thomas Linacre, and Thomas More—all friends of Erasmus. The Florentine sculptor Pietro Torrigiano designed Henry VII's tomb (1515), but had no English followers, and in the visual arts generally, though they occasionally displayed Renaissance features, there was no understanding of the principles of Renaissance classicism. Humanism had little effect on Scotland. The three Scottish universities founded in the 15th century were wedded to medieval methods.

Art and architecture

Henry VIII's famous court painter Holbein was German, and the most humanistic painting of Elizabeth's reign was by Hans Eworth, a Fleming. Native English painting was largely confined to portraits. Outstanding were the exquisite, gem-like miniature portraits of Nicholas Hilliard (1547–1619) and others, which though realistic, derived from the tradition of medieval illuminated manuscripts.

Great houses like Longleat in Wiltshire often incorporated Renaissance features, but no English architect fully understood the principles of Italian Renaissance architecture until Inigo Jones, in the 17th century.

Miniature portrait of James VI, who became James I of England.

The Queen's House in Greenwich, near London, by Inigo Jones (1616) was the first true Renaissance building in England (it is now part of the National Maritime Museum.)

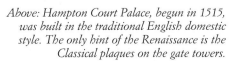

Above: Hampton Court Palace, begun in 1515, was built in the traditional English domestic style. The only hint of the Renaissance is the Classical plaques on the gate towers.

Medieval traditions

Among the most popular forms of fiction, in prose and poetry, was the medieval romance (so-called because it was written originally in Romance languages such as Italian and French). The subject is love and chivalry, with unlikely events set in an imaginary, idealized setting, often involving the hero in a quest. Famous examples were Ariosto's *Orlando Furioso* (1532) and Edmund Spenser's *The Faerie Queen* (1590s). The epic poem is similar but usually concerned with a heroic warrior rather than a lovesick knight, and derived from the heroes of Homer and Virgil. Examples were the Italian Tasso's *Gerusalemme Liberata* (1575) and Camoëns's great Portuguese national epic *Os Lusiadas* (1572), which celebrates the creation of the Portuguese empire, while suggesting doubts about imperialism.

Left: Illustration from the Spanish romance Amadis of Gaule (1508) *by Garcia Ordóñes de Montalvo which, in translations, became a European bestseller.*

Poets

Poetry in the Renaissance was still believed to have a moral purpose, as in ancient times, and poets were numerous, ranging from popes and queens to nuns and servants. In Italy, apart from Ariosto, poetry of the High Renaissance never equalled Dante and Petrarch. Lyric poetry flourished in France and other countries. Garcilaso de la Vega was the greatest poet of Spain's golden age. Another international favorite was the *Ship of Fools* (1494) by the German humanist Sebastian Brant, which mocks human foolishness.

Among many women poets was Vittoria Colonna, whose friendship inspired Michelangelo.

Literature and Drama

Modern European literature in all its many forms dates from the Renaissance. The new spirit of inquiry associated with humanism and the revival of Classical culture was probably the most important influence. Further stimulus came in the 16th century from the religious Reformation and the discovery of new lands. The new spirit of freedom encouraged a broadening of literary horizons and the ending of the dominance of religion. Even so, religious books continued to be written, and the Bible was the bestselling book. But the Bible, along with other books, appeared in current languages (not just Latin). And far more people could read and write, which, together with the crucial invention of printing, created a vastly larger market for books of all kinds, from profound scholarship to lightweight entertainment.

Fiction

The craze for unrealistic romances inspired the Spanish poet and playwright Miguel de Cervantes to write a mocking parody of that type of story. The result was *Don Quixote* (1605), the adventures of an elderly, idealistic but half-cracked knight and his down-to-earth squire, Sancho Panzo. It was one of the most successful novels ever written and made him perhaps Spain's greatest literary figure. While plenty of prose fiction was written, it was generally in the tradition of Boccaccio—tales, rather than novels. In England, John Lyly's *Euphues* (1578) gave the language a new word, euphuism, meaning overly elaborate and elegant language.

Cervantes (1547–1616), author of The History of the Valorous and Witty Knight-Errant Don Quixote.

France

The other great comic genius of the Renaissance was François Rabelais, a writer who seems, like his characters, larger than life. Rabelais (died about 1533) wrote learned works on medicine in Latin, but he is remembered for his comical, coarse, immensely lively tales of the popular giants Gargantua and Pantagruel. This vast collection mixed often-crude stories with extraordinary learning. Another French genius, Montaigne (1533–1592), was a total opposite. A country gentleman of great learning, common sense, humor, and tolerance, he wrote wonderfully wise essays in beautiful French that influenced hundreds of later writers, including Shakespeare.

Like artists, writers often depended on rich patrons. Here, Rabelais presents a copy of Pantagruel *(1532) to his patron, Cardinal du Bellay.*

Theaters

In Spain, the courtyards of charity hospitals provided the most useful performing area for acting companies. In England, inns, with their galleried buildings ranged around a courtyard, played the same part. The first custom-built public theaters developed from these buildings and, like them, were in the open air. The Globe (below) was an early London theater used by Shakespeare's company. The best seats were in the galleries; the pit was cheap but there was standing room only. In Italy, the first theaters followed Roman models, soon replaced by the familiar plan of a rectangular auditorium with a stage framed like a picture at one end—and a roof! The Teatro Farnese, in Parma (1618), had elaborate stage machinery for special effects.

Actors and playwrights

Medieval drama consisted of religious plays, performed in church, and mystery plays, performed in the marketplace by guilds. Groups of traveling entertainers performed at fairs and in great houses. The modern theater grew from these roots. Plays, especially comedies, were written for private patrons and court entertainments, later for public companies. The most fertile playwright was Lope de Vega (1562–1635), 500 of whose plays survive. By the 15th century, non-religious drama in current languages was taking national forms in many countries. Companies of actors were employed by monarchs or magnates. One of the first permanent, professional companies was run by Lope de Rueda (died 1565), Spain's first impresario, who wrote plays for his company.

William Shakespeare (1564–1623), England's greatest playwright, wrote tragedies (in verse) and comedies (in prose) for the company in which he was a minor actor.

An actor from the Italian commedia del'arte, a hugely influential form of comedy with fixed characters (Harlequin, Columbine, Pierrot) but no fixed script.

Germany

Although there was little popular literature or public theater in the Middle Ages, there were strong traditions of entertainment by minstrels, jesters, and traveling players. The *meistersingers*, or master singers, were poet-musicians who flourished in 16th-century Germany, but they belonged to a tradition going far back into the Middle Ages. They were ordinary people, members of guilds, who had elaborate rules for their art of song and held regular competitions. The most extraordinary of them was Hans Sachs (1494–1576) of Nuremburg, a practicing shoemaker, who wrote about 4,000 songs and 200 popular plays in verse, to be performed at fairs and carnivals.

A 16th-century woodcut of a scene from The Wandering Scholar *(1550), by Hans Sachs, the best-known of his popular dramas.*

Index